AF484856

MISSISSIPPI

Hippie

A Life in 49 Pieces

by
Willy Bearden

Mississippi Hippie, A Life in 49 Pieces, is a work of literature.

This book is a memoir. It reflects the author's present recollections of experiences over time. Some names and characteristics have been changed, some events have been compressed, and some dialogue has been recreated.

This is a book of memory, and memory has its own story to tell. But I have done my best to make it tell a truthful story.

I have tried to recreate events, locales, and conversations from my memories of them. In order to maintain their anonymity in some instances I have changed the names of individuals and places, I may have changed some identifying characteristics and details such as physical properties, occupations, and places of residence.

This book, in part, is a work of fiction. This book is a combination of facts about Willy Bearden's life and certain embellishments. Names, dates, places, events, and details have been changed, invented, and altered for literary effect. The reader should not consider this book anything other than a work of literature.

All rights reserved. This book or parts thereof may not be reproduced in any form, stored in any retrieval system, or transmitted in any form by any means—electronic, mechanical, photocopy, recording, or otherwise—without prior written permission of the publisher, except as provided by United States of America copyright law. For permission requests, contact William Bearden, PO Box 41135 Memphis TN 38174.

The Library of Congress Control Number 2024906477
Photographic illustrations by the author.
ISBN 979-8-9904023-0-0

Edited by Kim Bearden
Copy editing by Sheena Barnett
Body typeface: Baskerville 13 pt.
First edition, 2024
Copyright © 2024 by William Meredith Bearden (1950)
Visit my website at www.mississippihippiebook.com

"No one is ever free until they tell the truth about themselves and the life into which they've been cast. Write it down; tell it to a friend in need, or a stranger who needs diversion. We are all here to be a witness to something, to be of some aid and direction to other people."

-Tennessee Williams

Dedicated to Dudley Davis and Grace Young
who saw something in me and did something about it.

Contents

Acknowledgments

People have been so kind to me. I owe a debt of gratitude to all those who took a moment to answer my questions, give an opinion, or provide a word or two of encouragement. Over the past twenty years I've had the opportunity to speak to groups large and small, and I always urge people to encourage those around them. It is possibly the greatest gift one can give another person. So, in no specific order or line of reasoning, I thank the following people for who I've become. A little piece of you lives in me.

Kim Bearden, George Larrimore, David Tankersley, Tom Lonardo, Debbie Walker, William Walker, Doug Easley, John Buford, Jim Spake, Calvin Turley, Pam Parker Branham, Judy Card, Jimmy Ogle, Randy Chertow, Murray Riss, George Quarm, Darius Wallace, Tom Harris, Dan Murrell, Vickie Murrell, John and Vanessa Greenham, Mike Jones, Corey Parker, Bob Riseling, Antonio Quinn, John Pritchard, Perre Magness, Bob Nollner, Mike Cody, Bill Robison, Tom Thurmon, Scott Blake, Jane Roberts, Dennis Cryder, Andrew McDermott, Wayne Dowdy, Derrick Patterson, Eric Gales, Jay Sieleman, Priscilla Hernandez, Richard Prillaman, Wiley Brown, Rafe Murray, Kelsey Lyons, Jon Hornyak, Pat Mitchell, Steve Lockwood, Jimmy Tashie, Stanley Booth, Matthew Hasty, Ken Hall, Eddie Wilson, James Eddie Campbell, Lamar Sorrento, Shelley Baltz, Kevin Baltz, Jeff Bearden, Fran Bearden. You all have made my life richer just by being who you are.

Dr. Beverly Bond, Otis Sanford, Dr. Janann Sherman, Joe Lowry, Dr. Stephen Behrman, Anna Whalley, Mark Fleischer, Robin Salant, Thomas Melton, Les Dennie, Marsha Stone, John Matthews, Betsy Brackin, Zak Ozmo, Brent Taylor, Dr. Syed Azmi, Melanie White, Charlie Newman, Fletcher Golden, Jeanne

Seagle, Jay Wells, Tammy Parker, Virginia McLean, Jeanne Arthur, Steve Williams, Theresa Williams, Bob Barnett, Dale Schaefer, Sonny Hanback, Sheena Barnett, Linley Schmidt, Kelly Sowell, Roger Thompson, Susan "Cookie" Hatchett, Amanda Zorn, Michael Davis, Ward Archer, Henry Turley, Alex Turley, Blaine Baker, Jay Martin, Sandra Martin, Suzanne Hopper, Taryn Spake, Howard Stovall, Baylor Stovall, Charles Weissinger, Anne Weissinger, Mary Ann Weissinger Smith. I have gained so much by knowing each of you.

My children have become such fine human beings. Each of them is smart, compassionate, funny, empathetic, and insightful. I couldn't ask for anything more for them. Savannah Bearden, Matt Bearden, Maggie Bearden-Bracey, Dyanne Caldwell and Knight Caldwell, I love and respect and enjoy you all more than you'll ever know. My sons-in-law, Danny Bader and Main Bracey are two of the finest people I know. Carol and Bob Durdin, Courtney McCollum, Marlin Mayo, Henry Lovins, Josh and Shana Durdin, and Jack and Carly McBride, are the people who welcomed me into their family and have been such a pleasure to know and love.

The people I've played music with in my life have brought me joy and frustration and hope. George Quarm and Eddie Wilson were in my first band, even though we couldn't play any instruments. We stood there in my bedroom at ten and eleven years old, pantomiming the Kingston Trio, the Rooftop Singers, Elvis Presley, and Fats Domino. We spent long summer afternoons learning the words to every song. It was important to us. My next band was the Answers: Ken DeCell, Buster Herman, Charles Wesley, Johnny French, and sometimes a reluctant Hal DeCell III. His dad made him play with us. I was fourteen at the time. The No Name Band was next with Charles Ray Tilghman, Joe Jones, Bill Gray, and Tommy Williams. Next came another unnamed band, we only performed once, but it was great. Phyllis Bounds sat in on vocals that night: Robert Waldon, Johnny Waldon, and Ken

DeCell. The Columbus Flood Band came next in 1976, while I lived in Jackson, Mississippi for the longest six months of my short life: Carl Thornhill, Lance Young, David Lentz, Charlie Perkins. Tommy "Possum" Percival and Bill Gray were our roadies. We played lots of fraternity parties at the University of Southern Mississippi and some country music joints even though we didn't know but a handful of country tunes. A couple of years later, Lance Young, David Durrett and I formed a trio in Memphis. We played at the Daily Planet and the Cosmic Cowboy to the drunkest crowds I've ever witnessed. Fights and mayhem were the order of the day. I wrote songs for many years with Don Miller and Ronnie Bearman. They were successful country music songwriters. I never got anything cut, but I did get to go to Nashville many times to cut demos with some great musicians. That was a huge education.

I took a break for many years and then got talked into playing in a new band when I was fifty two. It was the GrayHounds, and for the next ten years we played in the Delta and the Ouachita Mountains of Arkansas. Those were some of the best times I can remember: Clark Secoy, Robert Waldon, Keith Carmack, Jerry Lambert, David Durrett, Jim Logan, and Robert Beaver. We could make anybody dance, and did. The old boys at the Elks Club in Mena, Arkansas loved us, as did the multitudes at the Great Delta Bear Affair in Rolling Fork, where we closed the festival for ten or so years. We played private parties, wedding receptions, and birthdays and had a ball. I made so many lifelong friends in Arkansas. Looking at you, Gopher, Bub, and Hoot.

I started playing with some guys in Memphis around 2006. We had been jamming at my building every now and again, and Russell George, who owned the Earnestine & Hazel's joint on South Main, would come over and bring Soul Burgers and listen and dance to us. Russell was a legendary dancer and the coolest guy in Memphis. He kept telling us that we were better than any band he ever paid, so why didn't we play at E&H. We began playing there for the Art

Walk/Trolley Night the last Friday of every month. That led to lots of other gigs, mainly private. I've been so fortunate to play with those great musicians for the last fifteen or so years. I have learned so much from each of them and forged some of the strongest friendships of my life: Doug Easley, Robert "Nighthawk" Tooms, John McClure, Calvin Turley, John Lightman, Gary Topper, and Tom Clary. What a time we've had. Up, down, and around. I'm still at it with these guys. We just played a couple of days ago. Music is the glue to so many of my relationships. I would be a poorer person in so many ways if I didn't participate in "Lodge Night" with John Buford, Jimmy Tashie, and Steve Lockwood. Our monthly meetings are the best. I will always owe a great debt of gratitude to John Kilzer for inviting me into this group.

I wish I could name everyone I've worked with. My Motion Picture Lab family is still so present and dear to me. All the people who have worked with and for me over the years have brought me so much pleasure and knowledge. I guess I can end this by thanking everyone I've ever known. Each of you has made me who I am.

Willy Bearden
November 14, 2023

The Book of the Dead

Willy and Jeff Bearden, 1962

I once kept a list of everyone I knew who had died. I was eleven. I began the list in the back of a spiral-bound composition notebook I kept hidden under a bookcase in my small bedroom. That act of secreting it spoke much about my life. I lived with shame and deflection and fantasy all spinning around my head like a cloud of mosquitoes or honeybees, everything trying to get my attention, trying to set me off in another direction. My present was chaotic, my prospects grim in the little house filled with resentment, regret, and joylessness. But the list, ah, how I felt a sense of pride and self worth in the act of compiling a list of those who had gone before me. I began the list with the people I didn't remember, but who had died while I was alive, and I kept on till I was caught up to the present day. Both my grandfathers, one of my grandmothers, my uncle John, and Miss Petty. Miss Petty Meek Kelly was the first dead person's hair Mama ever fixed. I know, because she paid me a quarter to go up to the funeral home with her and sit in the office while she did a shampoo and set on the recently passed Miss Petty. She even painted her fingernails.

The list went on like that, giving thought to the obvious as well as the hidden. I had to be vigilant about looking in the county newspaper every week to see who had died so I would be sure to add them to the list. My rule was that if I had ever seen them in person and knew who they were, then they qualified to go on the list. I quickly filled up two sheets in the notebook. It became almost a game to me. Every time we'd go to my grandmother's house, I'd inquire as to who had passed since the last time we'd been there and then ask her if I had ever met them. There seemed to be more deaths in the red clay hills of Mississippi than in our part of the Delta. The notion that someone was no longer here to be seen and heard but still very much alive in our minds fascinated me. Many years later, I still think about those not in attendance.

Nobody ever knew about the list till that one day my mother saw me writing in the notebook, and when I quickly tried to hide it from her, she snatched it from me and took it into the living room. After about five minutes called me in. She was concerned that I kept such a list. She kept asking me why, with this sad look on her face, but I didn't have an answer. I just wanted to know how many people

I knew or had known who were no longer alive. I know she thought I was turning out to be a weird kid and probably that she and my absent father had a lot to do with it, but I didn't stop making the list. I just hid it better.

It's crazy, but even though it has been almost sixty years, I could probably think hard and start the list back up if I wanted. It wouldn't be that difficult to go through the times of my life and figure out who was dead. I have an excellent memory. I can't think of the logic in this, but it might make a good screenplay: a guy goes through his life keeping a list of everyone around him who has died. Does he think that he'll see them all in heaven? Does it strengthen his faith? Destroy his faith? Does he begin to cheat and make up people? Does he become completely delusional? Does he question friends and use their friends and family to add to the list? Does he get a job working with the elderly and keep the list as a purely compassionate enterprise? And in the best Hollywood rationale, he could find his true love working in a nursing home. Does he go totally off the deep end and begin killing people just to add to the list? Now, that's the real Hollywood take. Hmm, many possibilities. If I ever get back to screenwriting, this might be worth taking a swing at.

The point of all this is that as I look at the hundred thousand-odd words I've written on this book in the past few years, much of it has to do with death and the people who were formerly in attendance. I somehow look to them, or maybe my ever-evolving understanding of them, to guide, measure, grieve, celebrate, and to learn from. COVID and age have taken so many of our friends and acquaintances that it is hard to remember sometimes who is here and not here. This reminds me of a video tribute I had to produce for the Blues Hall of Fame many years ago. Stevie Ray Vaughn was being inducted into the Hall, and a blues fan in California had offered to get a video clip of the great bluesman John Lee Hooker saying something about Stevie. We were to present it at this big show we were producing at the Kennedy Center in Washington, D.C. After many phone calls and not a little anxiety on my part, I finally got the videotape the day before the show. I found a video editing facility in Arlington, VA, and headed over to finish the tribute. I sat in the edit suite and listened to about twenty minutes of John Lee rambling about the blues but not saying much, or certainly anything usable about Stevie. The editor was looking uncomfortable, and finally told me he hadn't understood a word John Lee had said. I laughed, and was glad I had grown up beside many "John Lees." I understood what he was saying, but still there wasn't anything that was perfect for what I needed. I was thinking that I might have to go to Plan B (at this point, there was no Plan B), when John Lee sat up straight, looked at the camera and said loudly, "Stevie Ray, he gone, but he ain't gone." I thought that was one of the most profound statements I had ever heard. These many years later, I often think about that statement from an old man because every person I've known and loved, though they may be gone, they are still right here with me. Their resonance, though diminished, or maybe transformed, is still in my ear, my memory, and my heart. Gone, but not gone.

This book is for everyone I've ever loved. It is also a book for everyone I've ever hated, feared, dismissed, ridiculed, praised, envied, or any of a thousand feelings. In the end, I hope it's about growth and forgiveness. Those are great aspirations but sometimes hard to accomplish.

You will read stories filled with humor, heartbreak, longing, regret, and joy. All are true to some degree. I know people will wonder who is who, where things actually happened, and to what degree fiction has been employed. I will answer simply that everything herein happened.

In Praise of the Hippie

The Answers, the second-best band in Rolling Fork, Mississippi. L to r, Charles Wesley, Hall DeCell, III, Willy Bearden, Ken DeCell, Buster Herman.
Photo by Hal DeCell, II

A couple of years ago, my wife jokingly called me her "Mississippi Hippie." We got a good chuckle out of that, but we realized it was as true an observation of me as anyone had ever made. I have wondered many times why I recognized my life experiences as a series of lessons in justice, empathy, and kindness. I question if I was actively looking for life lessons or if those lessons were looking for me.

In today's world people are intimidated and literally scared to death of what they call "woke" culture. It is presented as some malevolent force, bent on stealing something that is divinely ours, and by ours, I mean white people, and by extension, evangelical Christians. Any attempt to bring people of different backgrounds or social standing together is met with cries of what used to be called race mixing. Attacks on other intrusions to the order of our society ranged from the hip-shaking of Elvis Presley to the long hair and liberal ideas of the Beatles.

This is the thing I was confronted with as a ninth grader in Rolling Fork. We had put together a little band called The Answers. (I'll go ahead and head off any commentary by stating that, no, we didn't even know the question). The name was given to us by Hal DeCell, a known liberal and the editor of our town's weekly newspaper, The Deer Creek Pilot, a publication which has been in business and relevant since 1886. In addition to having a cross burned in his front yard, Mr. DeCell was also the father of our guitarist and singer, Ken DeCell, as well as Hal DeCell, III, who was begrudgingly pressed into service as our saxophonist. The band caused quite a stir the day we played for the assembly at our school. Immediately after the two song performance, the football coaches called us into their office in the gymnasium and told us in no uncertain terms that the playing of Beatles songs was a direct affront to everything a Colonel (our team mascot) stood for. The coaches had surely seen the nearly universal uproar caused by the Fab 4 on their recent appearance on the Ed Sullivan TV program. The big, scary world was creeping in on our little corner in the Mississippi Delta. It was clear, to me at least, that nothing was ever to be the same.

Young people were rejecting the rigid conformity of the 1950s, embracing individuality and freedom of expression. This spirit of nonconformity encouraged creativity and independent thinking.

While it may have been perceived as unconventional and countercultural at the time, it brought forth several positive aspects that continue to influence society today.

The hippie movement was synonymous with the spirit of love. The emphasis on love and harmony promoted unity among diverse groups of people. The "Make love, not war" slogan reflected the desire for a more peaceful world, and that resonated with many young people tired of the Vietnam War and the Cold War tensions.

Hippies were often at the forefront of advocating for ecological sustainability. Their back-to-nature ethos and protests against pollution and deforestation laid the foundation for today's environmental activism.

The alternative culture also played a major role in the civil rights and social justice movements. Many young people took part in protests for racial equality, women's rights, and LGBTQ+ rights, championing inclusivity and equality for all.

The era produced a surge in experimental art and music, an explosion of creativity and cultural innovation.

Rejecting materialism and consumerism, hippies promoted a simpler way of life. This mindset encouraged people to prioritize experiences, relationships, and personal growth over material possessions, a perspective that remains relevant today.

The era was marked by an appreciation for cultural diversity. Eastern philosophies, indigenous traditions, and world music all found their way into the mainstream. This cultural fusion enriched society's tapestry and broadened people's horizons. The idea of there being more than one way to God or spirituality was a life-saving surprise for so many of my contemporaries who struggled through the noise of the different brands of religion we were faced with. *Better not dance. Drinking is the road to eternal damnation. Ours is the "real" religion. Don't trust what the Methodists tell you, or the Presbyterians.*

It didn't take long for the movement to become co-opted, misrepresented, and misunderstood by both the news media and the political establishment in America. They were scared, and scared people will do anything to hold onto whatever power they think they need.

The news media often focused on the sex, drugs, and rock 'n' roll, rather than its deeper philosophies and ideals. This sensationalism tended to overshadow the movement's more profound messages of peace, love, and social change.

Some elements of the counterculture, like tie-dye clothing and long hair, were picked up by the mainstream fashion industry. This commercialization diluted the movement's authenticity.

Politicians and the political establishment sometimes tried to co-opt the energy of the counterculture for their own purposes. They made efforts to appeal to young voters by adopting a more relaxed and informal style, even if their policies didn't align with countercultural values.

The political establishment, particularly the FBI under J. Edgar Hoover, viewed the counterculture with suspicion. Law enforcement agencies conducted surveillance on activists and organizations, often lumping them together with extremist or radical groups.

While drug use was prevalent within the counterculture, it's inaccurate to label the entire movement as drug-centric. Many activists and members of the counterculture were critical of the negative effects of substance abuse and advocated for responsible drug use.

The counterculture's anti-establishment stance led some to perceive its members as unpatriotic or anti-American. However, many activists saw their actions as a form of patriotism, pushing for a more just and equitable society and challenging what they saw as the government's unjust policies.

Sensationalism, cultural appropriation, and misunderstandings about the movement's core values all contributed to these misconceptions. While there were certainly elements of the counterculture that matched some stereotypes, it's essential to recognize the diversity and complexity of the individuals and ideas within the movement. Many counterculture members were deeply committed to social change, peace, and love, and their contributions had a lasting impact on American society and culture.

I am proud of my hippie roots.

Foundations

Willy & Jeff Bearden, Easter, 1953

We all have foundational stories that run the width and breadth of our lives, haunting, calling out, informing, visiting us in our quiet moments, calming or fanning the fires of our insecurities. They are always present, real and authentic, our own unique melody. Some might call them the voice of God, whispering and nudging our every move, every thought, every breath. I believe our learned reactions to these experiences are what separates creativity from intellectual shyness, magnanimity from selfishness, and greatness from degeneracy. Children who live in chaos are far more likely to perpetuate chaos. The endless circle of poverty, alcohol and drug abuse, domestic violence, and hopelessness are common stories in our society, but it's more than the lack of money or access to education and basic human services. There is a sickness of the soul that manifests in selfishness, suspicion, greed, and a hundred other maladies that infect everyone involved. Those around an abuser are destined to struggle with finding a way out of the madness or becoming a monster themselves. Many times that struggle is the defining life experience of generations of families.

These days, there's a name for this condition. It's called Adverse Childhood Experiences, or ACE. Here's the quiz from the CDC to find out if you might suffer from ACE.

These ten confidential questions provide your warning signs.

Question 1 of 10

Before your 18th birthday, did a parent or other adult in the household often or very often...

swear at you, insult you, put you down, or humiliate you?

or

act in a way that made you afraid that you might be physically hurt? Yes No

Question 2 of 10

Before your 18th birthday, did a parent or other adult in the household often or very often...

push, grab, slap, or throw something at you?

or

ever hit you so hard that you had marks or were injured? Yes No

Question 3 of 10

Before your 18th birthday, did an adult or person at least five years older than you ever...

touch or fondle you or have you touch their body in a sexual way?

or

attempt or actually have oral, anal, or vaginal intercourse with you? Yes No

Question 4 of 10

Before your 18th birthday, did you often or very often feel that...

no one in your family loved you or thought you were important or special?

or

your family didn't look out for each other, feel close to each other, or support each other? Yes   No

Question 5 of 10

Before your 18th birthday, did you often or very often feel that...

you didn't have enough to eat, had to wear dirty clothes, and had no one to protect you?

or

your parents were too drunk or high to take care of you or take you to the doctor if you needed it? Yes No

Question 6 of 10

Before your 18th birthday, was a biological parent ever lost to you through divorce, abandonment, or other reason? Yes No

Question 7 of 10

Before your 18th birthday, was your mother or stepmother:

often or very often pushed, grabbed, slapped, or had something thrown at her?

or

sometimes, often, or very often kicked, bitten, hit with a fist, or hit with something hard?

or

ever repeatedly hit over at least a few minutes or threatened with a gun or knife? Yes No

Question 8 of 10

Before your 18th birthday, did you live with anyone who was a problem drinker or alcoholic, or who used street drugs? Yes No

Question 9 of 10

Before your 18th birthday, was a household member depressed or mentally ill, or did a household member attempt suicide? Yes No

Question 10 of 10

Before your 18th birthday, did a household member go to prison? Yes No

Your ACE score is:

Getting Started

And so, I begin with the story that has made me, and I have presented it as true as I can tell it. The funny thing is that I wrote it in 1984, in a rush, after I saw a flyer at a bookstore announcing the River City Writers Conference to be held at Southwestern College (now Rhodes) in Memphis, that coming July. The conference was to be a gathering of known writers who would teach classes each morning for a week and participate in readings each evening. Larry McMurtry, Howard Nemerov, Barry Hannah, Shirley Abbott, Gordon Osing, and other writers were to be there in the flesh, accessible, and hopefully approachable. The only problem was the conference fee was a whopping $350, a lot of money at the time. But as fate would have it, I saw another flyer at the Peabody library a few days later announcing that a full scholarship would be given to the person who wrote the best piece of short fiction or nonfiction. As I read and re-read the flyer I knew that I was going to write a story good enough to win a ticket to what seemed to me the best week I could imagine, and I had just the story. Although I had been writing for several years, mostly poetry and futile attempts at short stories, I had never written 3,000 words at one time, but that didn't bother me at all. I went home, sandwiched a sheet of typing paper, a piece of carbon paper, and another sheet in my 1960s-era Adler typewriter, and began writing. When I looked up a few hours later, I was done. I put the manuscript in the mail the next day and waited. Sure enough, after a couple of weeks, I got a nice letter from the poet, Gordon Osing, informing me that I had won the scholarship to that year's conference. As I look back, thirty-eight years later, it was a magical week of listening to other writers (I gave permission to call myself a writer for that week) say out loud so many of the things I was thinking, so many of the fears I possessed, and many of the goals and dreams I had kept to myself, thinking they were outlandish or even delusional. Here's the story I wrote. Here's even a photograph of the first page out of the Adler.

William Bearden
1752 Lawrence
Memphis, TN 38112
728-4490

REUNION

I never thought to question why he was so different from
other men. Even when I'd overhear other school kids talking
about him in hushed, sniggering tones, looking surprised when
they knew I was near, I thought it was as it should be. Like
someone had given him a permanent "time out"; like the rules
were for everyone else but him. So, it stands to reason that
I was not surprised in the least the day those two men brought
him home.

I had not seen him in almost a month but that month had taken
an incredible toll on my father. What until now had been the
complacent, resigned look of an alcoholic had turned wild
and frantic as if some demon inhabited his skinny 130 pound
frame. His eyes darted from street to car to house and back
again as the two strangers held onto his arms helping him
out of his car. The big '59 Buick had the telltale red dust

1

Reunion

I had not seen him in almost a month, but that month had taken an incredible toll on my father. What until now had been the complacent, resigned look of an alcoholic had turned wild and frantic as if some demon inhabited his skinny 130-pound frame. His eyes darted from street to car to house and back again as the two strangers held onto his arms helping him out of his car. The big '59 Buick had the telltale red dust from the central Mississippi hill country. Mud was splashed on the fenders. I remember looking at the dust and mud for a long time thinking he must be really sick to let his car get so dirty. Despite all his bad traits, he was fastidious to an almost maniacal degree when it came to his car. He might get drunk every day and run around with the scum of the earth but his car was always spotless.

One of the men, the one with black wavy hair sort of roached up on his head, called out to me and asked was 'this where Bill lived?'. Actually, what he said, gruffly, was, "You Bill's boy?" I answered that I was, wondering why he had asked such an obvious question while being right there in the company of my father. As they led him up the front walk, I noticed he didn't know where he was. He was looking around like he was at the state fair in Jackson making his first stroll down the midway. He was saying something under his breath as they were walking into the house. Almost mumbling, he spoke slowly and quietly about trains and people coming to get him. The two men walked him right through the living room and into the bedroom I shared with my brother. My father got into Benny's bed, with all his clothes on, even his boots. He pulled the covers all the way up to his chin.

Then, as quickly as they had come, the two men left. I followed them to the door, asking in my ten-year-old way what was wrong; they just said he was sick. It was then that I noticed the other car. It too had hill dust that we weren't used to seeing in the delta. Behind the wheel was a woman with sunglasses, lots of makeup, and black teased-up hair; the kind of woman I always connected with Nashville and beer joints. She was looking around nervously as if she was in a hurry to leave. Both men got into the car and the woman drove away without even looking at me.

It was almost noon, a distant dinner bell from the farm on the other side of the railroad tracks called the field hands to their lunches of rag bologna, soda crackers, sweaty orange and grape drinks, stage planks and moon pies. I stood there in the front yard staring at where the hill car had been, wanting to run to town to get somebody... Mama, or Mr. Boob McCaa, or Mr. Pete Brown. Somebody who would know what to do.

On the other side of town, out by the highway, the men who lived on the counter stools at the Plantation View restaurant fueled the conversation with coffee and 8-ounce cokes and talked of crops and rain. The dust was so thick on the cotton the fields looked as if they were covered with snow. Crops were laid by and needed an occasional rain and plenty of hot humid days to make the bolls open like white roses come fall and the first frost. Across the dusty parking lot, in back of the ice house, the same conversation was taking place among the boys who were mostly white trash and didn't rate a stool in the restaurant proper.

They worked at the service station and ice house for the owner of both establishments, Clyde Breedlove. Clyde, most likely, was laid up in his trailer behind the Plantation View with his new wife, Carol Sue. The object of the majority of adolescent fantasies in that part of the delta, Carol Sue was the thirty-five-year-old mother of three of the meanest, nastiest talking, sassiest kids to ever draw breath. But Carol Sue, ah, Carol Sue. The raw sex of the woman was evident to every man in the county. She could melt the heart of any man with those green eyes. Dangerous in her short shorts, she caused a commotion just by walking down the street. Many a man had received a death stare from his wife when Carol Sue was around.

The boys in back of the icehouse began a slow game of throwing ice picks toward a bullseye drawn on the wooden planks of the building. The conversation in the house grew louder and louder. I tried to sneak to the bedroom door.

He saw me before I could run out of the house. He asked me to get his cigarette lighter out of his shirt pocket. The shirt had been hung on the post of the bunk bed by one of the men. As I reached inside the shirt pocket I thought hours must have passed since the men and the woman in sunglasses had driven off. I knew it had been only minutes. It was like trying to remember Christmas, the image was there but the details had slipped away like the sun on a February afternoon. The lighter was neither in his shirt pocket nor his pants pockets. I had not overlooked it. I knew that lighter as well as I knew my birthday, a clear Ronson with a fish hook floating in the fluid. I told him he must have dropped it somewhere. He looked at me with disbelief. That was the fifteenth lighter he had lost that day, he said. Then he began to rail about all the thieves around and how nothing was safe anymore. He sat straight up in the bed and looked past me and began talking to someone I could not see. He went on and on about how the person was trying to get him and put him on a midnight train and carry him away. There was something bad wrong. I had always associated "crazy" with Mama's brother's first wife, Maude Fay. Uncle Layton was quite a few years older than Mama, so when he married Maude Fay and moved into a tenant house on Grandpaw's place, they took Mama in as their own; treating her like a little six-year-old queen. But a scratch, a minor thing she hardly noticed, from one of her pet cats, turned Maude Fay into a crazy woman. It took three strong men to hold her down till they could get the straight jacket on her and take her to the state hospital at Whitfield. The next day they called Uncle Layton and said Maude Fay had died during the night.

I had lived my ten years with this vision of crazy without really questioning the details; a straight jacket, Whitfield, and death. I began to cry. There was nothing else to do but run uptown and get Mama.

When I walked into the beauty shop the ladies under the dryers were occupied with Photoplay magazine and the duller McCalls and Redbook. I read Photoplay religiously and believed everything about Liz and Debbie and Eddie and Richard. I finished putting my shirttail in as I reached Mama's booth. She was fixing old Mrs. Noble's hair into those tight little waves that old ladies always wear. It was Friday, I knew Mrs. Noble would make me eat one of her peach tarts she always brought. I didn't like peaches and much less her "sputniks," little tarts shaped like flying saucers that tasted too much like old lady stuff for me. Mama asked if I had finished with the hedges. I told her that some men had brought Daddy home and that he was sick. I walked back to the little closet where they kept the bottles of shampoo and clean towels and motioned for her to come. I told her as best I could what had happened and how Daddy was acting. She didn't seem to be very concerned. I could see that she was already tired. With six hours left in her long day she was in no mood to play nursemaid to a man who had let her down too many times. She told me to get back home and call her if he got worse. I could tell she just thought that he was more drunk than usual. He had been down in Vicksburg for a month without coming home and had drunk himself into a stupor.

I didn't want to go home. I sat on the footbridge looking down into the slow green water of Deer Creek, I walked through a vacant lot; hot johnsongrass sawed at my bare legs. As I passed Charlie Cartwright's house he motioned from his garden for me to come over. Charlie was a Black man in his late sixties with the lines of his years so evident on his face you could almost read his whole life story at a glance. Worn out from his years in the fields, Charlie was happy to work in his garden and spend the late summer afternoons sitting under his mimosa tree sipping buttermilk from a Ball jar. He gave me a mess of pole beans to take home and admonished me to have them snapped by the time Mama got home. It was common knowledge how hard she worked. While it was not his place to be telling me what to do, he and I had an understanding in our eyes that transcended race and even words. I took the paper sack of beans with me. I wanted to tell Charlie what was happening but I knew it would be wrong. Wrong for him to come into a white man's house and try to help. Wrong for him to witness what was clearly a private problem.

As I neared the house, I couldn't make myself go in. I stood out front for what seemed an eternity. I just couldn't go inside. I could hear him getting louder and louder, and more frightening. I ran. I ran over to the Illinois Central railroad tracks and sat down on the rail. I picked up handfuls of porous gray gravel and threw them at nothing. I walked down the tracks for a few yards and came back. I heard a commotion over on Bluefront, the negro street, and I saw him come through a backyard and out into the street. He had my baseball bat! Swinging and shaking the bat, he was screaming at the same person. Now the pitch had become feverish. He said he was ready to fight. He would not be taken without a fight. They would not get him on that train. No, he would die first. "Y'all gon have to kill me!" he shouted.

Someone must have called the Sheriff. I stood there with tears streaming down my face watching all the people, mostly negroes, gather around. We watched the sheriff try to calm him down, put the handcuffs on and finally place him in the car. The sheriff put him in the front seat, I don't know why I thought that was so odd... the front seat. But, of course, Mack Phillips and he were friends. They were in the Lions Club together. In fact, Mack was the Tail Twister when my father was secretary-treasurer. I was afraid. I wondered who had seen all this. Would Mr. Mack take him to jail? Whitfield? Whitfield, that far away place (outside Jackson) where they kept all the crazy people. The place children named in cruel jokes. I ran, knowing that I would be called upon to recount the day's events in other places, other times. I ran.

1962

February

The morning was still as an empty house. We woke up to a covering of snow on the ground. There would be no school on this Wednesday. Even if the buses could make it in from the country, snow was such a rarity everyone knew that this was an unofficial holiday.

I had only seen snow three times in my eleven years and that was counting the winter after I was born when Mama said we had a foot of snow on the ground for four days. I couldn't wait to get outside and feel the snow and maybe even build a snowman if there was enough. I put on my long underwear that had been dyed brown to accommodate my role as a monkey in the fifth-grade school play. We had oatmeal to eat. I put sugar and milk on mine and tried to get Mama to get dressed and go outside with me. Instead, she took me back to her bedroom and showed me a letter from my father. It said he was coming home. I didn't want to read the letter but I did it because she wanted me to. As I looked at her, I couldn't tell what she was thinking. Seven months was a long time for someone to be in Whitfield. The doctor said that he was just fine. They had tried several different treatments and it seemed that they had all been beneficial. The shock treatments had done their job....that's what the doctors had told Mama on her last trip to Whitfield. I later found out that my aunt, Daddy's sister and a wealthy woman, had asked Mama for gas money when she took her to Whitfield.

The snow was lost to me that day. I went through the motions of snowball fights and makeshift sledding but my heart was not in it. I knew that the bus from Vicksburg would pull into Cecil's service station and my father would walk back into our lives with little or no explanation of the things that had happened. These things that had pushed me from a child into that neutral ground of being neither a man nor a carefree child again. I hated that bus. That goddamn Vicksburg bus that I had listened to roaring along Deer Creek thousands of nights while I stood after supper at the burning garbage can. That Vicksburg bus I had wanted to take me away from this nowhere town to far off Memphis or St Louis. And I hated him for never letting me know all those things I had to figure out on my own. I hated him for being selfish, for being in Whitfield, for making me feel embarrassed at school.

I ate supper early that evening. The sun had slipped away before five o'clock, and the impending doom of my task lay before me worse than any report card or polio shot day. I was to escort Daddy home.

I knew better than to protest this...it would have done no good anyway.

I stood close to the trash can that evening trying to keep warm against the biting February wind and below-freezing temperatures. I thought I heard the Vicksburg bus coming every few seconds, but I knew it wasn't time yet. I sat on a Coke case alone in front of the darkened service station, I saw the lights of the Greyhound before I actually heard it. It was rounding the corner by the drugstore. It looked all alone coming down the snow-covered street. I remember thinking that no one was on the bus.

I was still sitting when the driver opened the door and came over to get the few packages that were in the big wooden chest behind me. Then, like an apparition, there he was standing at the bottom step in the door of the bus. I don't remember getting up, but I was hugging him and he was hugging me back. We walked home under meager streetlights.

Johnny Can't Read

Virginia Wright Bearden, c.1955

When I was about ten my mother sat me down after a particularly bad report card and asked me to read a story from the Jackson Daily News. We sat on the couch in our living room, right by the gas space heater. I can still see her sitting there, her legs propped on the coffee table, those legs in the white support hose she had to wear every day because her varicose veins were so bad. She'd had them stripped several years before, and had to wear Ace bandages for months and months, but standing on her feet for ten to twelve hours a day had only worsened the problem. I felt sorry for her, there alone with me, a dumbass who couldn't make passing grades, husband gone, working as a beautician six days a week, cupboards bare, yet having to worry that I couldn't read. She handed me the newspaper and asked me to read the story. I stumbled through a sentence or two before she stopped me. "You can't read, can you?"

"I can read Mama, that's just hard. That's the newspaper."

"You really can't read," she said quietly to herself, then tears filled her eyes and overflowed to her cheeks. She didn't move. We sat there for a long time and when she finally wiped her eyes with the end of her apron, she looked at me hard for a second and said, "Okay, now tomorrow you're going up to the library and you're going to get a book. I don't care if it's a third grade book, or even a second grade book, you're going to check out a book that you can read and you're going to read it. Don't let anyone see you with the book, I don't want you to be embarrassed, but you're going to come home and read that book. I don't care if it takes you a week. And you're going to get another book and read it too. And another one after that. I may not be able to do much to keep us alive, but I can make sure you know how to read."

Somebody had brought paper bags of groceries and put them on our back steps that morning. They were there when we woke up. My mother was so embarrassed but we ate the cereal and looked through the bags, pulling boxes and cans out with great relish, items and brands we had never treated ourselves to. Post Toasties and cans of Chef Boyardee spaghetti, and a Swan's Down cake mix. It was like Christmas morning. "I wonder who did this?" she asked, to no one in particular. We did OK after that. Somehow she started making a little more money and was able to pay the bills, and I worked at the Mansour's grocery store in the afternoons and on Saturdays. Mama never wanted to take my money but it did make life a little easier. It would be another two years before she met Joe and married him after a five-month courtship, but we never went hungry after that, and I read a book every week from that time on.

Not long ago, I found this book in a second hand bookstore, "Hot Rod" by Henry Gregor Felson. I almost cried when I saw it. Sixty years ago it was one of my proudest moments to finish a book that was considered "grade appropriate" for my age.

I had the book framed and hung it in the library in my house in Rolling Fork.

Grandmothers Against Divorce

The M.O. Wright Family, c.1926

After my parents divorced, it took a long time before my mother broke the news to my grandmother. She was of the old school and simply didn't believe in divorce. She truly believed a woman should stay with her man no matter what. She believed in God and that's what God said in the Bible. I also think she secretly thought my mother was spoiled and somewhat of a complainer. Mama had been the baby of the family for about seven years, and she apparently ruled the roost, as they say. I don't think anyone understood the depth of selfishness and mental abuse my father caused.

There is a studio photograph, taken in 1925 or '26, of my mother's whole family, and you can just feel the tension from the looks on everyone's face. It seems that the drive to the studio took almost three hours in a Ford Model A, over muddy Mississippi roads, my mother throwing tantrum after tantrum the whole way. In the photograph, my mother is seated by her father, who has her hand clamped in his, as she sits there with her head lolled to one side, looking like the brat she was that day long ago. Her siblings sport tight smiles that speak volumes. My grandmother looks almost through the camera with a resolve that became her look for the balance of her life. She could not, would not, concede defeat on any level. Her steadfast faith was her crutch, her solace, her sustenance, and she was going to stick to that come hell or high water. A lot of what happened in the 60s and 70s killed that kind of thinking in Mississippi and probably other places as well, but my parents' actual divorce didn't change much. My father still came to Rolling Fork one weekend a month as if nothing had happened.

Shirley

I bought a house in Rolling Fork in 2003, and had been visiting every few weeks, just settling in for a few months. I began asking around about a Black girl I knew when I was thirteen. Her name was Shirley. I didn't expect her to still live around here. I assumed she had beat it to Chicago or Detroit forty years ago. She was the kind of girl who would have done anything to get out. She had the moxie, or gumption as they called it back then, to get what she wanted. She came by it naturally. Her mother was the unofficial boss of the hoe-hands on the biggest plantation hereabouts, the Mound. It was called that because it comprised all the land surrounding a group of Indian mounds that overlooked Deer Creek. Lore among the local Black folks was that it was haunted and that anyone who owned it would come to a bad end. There were stories going back for decades of duels, disappearances, freak accidents, suicides, overdoses of pills and alcohol, and any number of heartbreaking circumstances. To say the place was haunted might be taking it too far, but maybe not. Anyway, I was thinking about Shirley when a friend told me she was still living in Rolling Fork. I wondered if she'd remember me if I ran into her at the grocery store.

The reason I had been thinking about Shirley was that I had written my first short story about her many years before. In many ways she was very much like me, and I felt an affinity with her every time she was around. Granted, in 1960s Mississippi, there weren't many times when a twelve-year-old white boy and his Black female counterpart were together, but in those times I seemed to notice her, watch her, and even understand her in some strange way. That story was my first attempt at reconciling the awful things we do to one another. It may be the most honest pack of lies I've ever written. I'll let you read it in the next chapter.

Let me state here and now that I am a huge proponent of reparations for Black people. Three hundred years of free labor to enrich a still-wealthy white population is the original sin of our country.

On a side note, every time I went to Rolling Fork, I would leave downtown Memphis at 5 or 6 and get to the house about 9 pm or so. By the time I put up the groceries I've bought at the Cleveland Walmart and turn on the air conditioners or heat, it's usually midnight. The house is quiet and I sleep soundly and contentedly. In retrospect, this house was a refuge for me, a place I could escape to from my then-present situation. I don't want to talk about all the things that were going sideways during that time, but trust me, it was ugly. The four or five days in Rolling Fork, though filled with writing and video editing work, offered a welcome respite from my reality.

The Foot Bridge

Looking south from the footbridge in Rolling Fork.

The day was hot, even for late June. The sky, not blue, but blank and monochrome, took on proportion and shape only as it met the earth at the far horizon. The omnipresent haze of the flat Delta waved and seemed nearly to pulsate in the otherwise mid-afternoon stillness. The field hands were far away from the pickup truck, but not nearly in the middle of the cotton field whose rows were over a mile long, their hoes rising and falling in no particular rhythm, but slow and without passion. The green '54 Ford was parked in the dank shade of a tall pecan tree along the bank of the slow-moving creek. Two white boys sat motionless in the dusty cab. They hadn't spoken in long minutes. The only sound was the occasional cry from the far distance of "waddo!" A brown horsefly bothered the boy sitting in the driver's seat. He swatted, unsuccessfully, and banged his hand on the side vent handle. "I'm gon kill that goddamn horsefly. Why don't we bring a fly swatter out here with us?" From two hundred yards away in the field, the cry arose, this time beginning as a single call, then rising like a church chorus, scattered and ill-defined, then finally into a collective call for "waddo."

"You goin'?" the first boy asked, still rubbing his hand.

"It's too hot," replied the other, smaller boy slumped in the passenger seat. "I just took 'em some not an hour ago. That's just Simmy gettin' everybody worked up. Anyway, it's your turn."

The driver smiled, "No it ain't, you said you'd tote all afternoon if I gave you that cigarette. You better get out there before they tell Mr. Rivers. Or Bojo might spit snuff in your face again." He smiled, knowing that would get a rise out of the other boy.

"That little sonofabitch tripped me, he didn't beat me."

"That's what you say, but I saw you were scared when he came after you. You looked scared."

"It was just 'cause he stunk so much, I didn't want him even touching me. Damn snuff juice all over his chin and smellin' like a hog."

"Them girls were sayin' Johnny Brown can beat you up."

"I'd like to see him try...he's a damn sissy."

The chorus in the distance waned, and the two boys sat in silence for what seemed like minutes although it was a much shorter time.

"Who's that?" the boy in the passenger seat said.

"Looks like Rena," said the driver.

"What's she doin'?"

"I don't know, maybe she's comin' to get the other file for Mr. Arthur. Is it behind the seat?"

"He's got that brand new file, and you know he ain't sharpenin' no damn hoe hot as it is. What the hell does she want?"

"You better get your ass out there and fill that bucket up...or she'll beat your ass. She ain't no Johnny Brown."

The other boy said nothing, but kept his eye on the steadily approaching girl. She was walking, no, dragging her bare feet through the dust of the Mississippi June cotton field. Down below the scorching surface inch of hot dust was the cool presence of the earth, the meager gift of relief in the otherwise brutal landscape.

The boy stood by the truck bed, thinking first to get the five-gallon galvanized water bucket and dipper out of the back and begin filling it from the 55-gallon drum filled with water and the once-huge, 50-pound block of ice they had bought from the ice house at 6 am that morning. The burlap bag, a "croker sack" in Delta parlance, sagged under its own weight and threatened to fall into the now lukewarm water. The boy looked at the water drum.

Rena continued her trudge across the field, moving slower now, her momentum hindered by the heat, but still coming ever closer. The boy shifted to lean against the bed of the pickup truck, then thought better of it. She was fifty yards away, and he needed to establish himself, his power, his position before she got there. When she saw that he was looking at her, she renewed her effort in the six-inch deep dust, dragging her feet more quickly now, creating a layer of hanging dust like ground fog on a November morning. He could sense that the work in the field had stopped, and every one of the more than fifty field hands were watching Rena's progress as she neared the pickup truck. The boy reached into the bed of the pickup and lifted out the bucket and dipper. Afraid to look in her direction, he busied himself with the bucket until he felt her presence behind him. He turned, shoving his hands in the pockets of his jeans and glaring at the young Black girl in front of him. In that moment, everything was quiet, only the dry scree of cicadas and the occasional deep croak from a frog in the nearby creek broke the uncomfortable silence. Rena was shaking, almost imperceptibly, but shaking nonetheless. They looked at one another for a long moment. Then, as if with the violent release of a scream, she slapped him with her sweaty open hand across the side of his head, catching his ear with a blow that exploded like a cherry bomb inside his head. He instinctively reached for his ear, but the momentum of the blow coupled with his fisted hands in the jeans, dropped him to the ground, the dust turning to a light film of mud as it mixed with his sweat. Tears stung his eyes in that instant, and he wanted nothing more than to lie on the ground in the cool dust and cry. She sprung as if to hit him again, and he brought his knees to his chest anticipating the blow that did not come. Then it was quiet again.

The other boy, now aware of the fight, jumped out of the truck, but did not approach the girl. "Rena, what in the hell are you doin'?"

She did not acknowledge his presence, but instead came a step closer to the boy on the ground, and through tears of intense anger said, "You been hearing us holler for water for near 'bout an hour now, and you ain't did nothin' but lay up in that truck. Now, goddamnit, when folks hollers for water, you better bring some goddamn water. My mama and them out there 'bout to fall out!" At that, she wheeled and began the long walk back to the still motionless group in the field. Moments later the boy had stood, brushed what dust he could from his shirt and pants, and began filling the bucket with water.

***

November

He watched from the corner of the drugstore and waited till he saw Josie walk up the steps into the beauty shop. He knew she had waited till the last minute to show up for work because she knew if he got there first his mama would have him begin sweeping up the day's volume of hair on the floor. "Sorry-ass Josie with three kids and not yet twenty years old," he thought, as he walked across the street. But that wasn't the half of it. She regularly told on him for the slightest indiscretions. She'd amble into the beauty shop, her hair a shock of steel wool, titties swinging beneath a dirty white t-shirt, run-over house shoes and a tight skirt, and whisper to his mama to come back in the storeroom where she'd tell of seeing the boy smoking a cigarette on the creek bank, or walking into the pool hall, or hanging around Jimmy's juke joint out on the creek road. She'd begin, "Miss Bernice, I know you havin' trouble raisin' them boys by yo'self, especially that Billy, and I know you don't want them getting into no trouble and carryin' on in the street around town, but I saw..." and on she'd go into the details of his latest transgression, his mother's lips turning to a taut line as she heard the story, knowing he'd deny everything when confronted later at home. But today Josie had no news to tell, and shuffled back to the storeroom, but not before slipping a Salem out of an open pack at the deserted front counter.

Bernice acknowledged Josie's presence by glancing at the clock, then went back to work. Three more shampoo and sets before she could go home. She stepped to the small table behind her station, took a bite of the sputnik, an apricot-filled flying saucer-shaped pastry one of her customers had brought earlier in the day, took a sip of the ever-present Coke, and stepped back to her booth where old Mrs. Pettaway sat, head halfway covered with tissue twisted papers held tightly with bobby pins to her nearly bald head. The old woman had fallen asleep in the brief time Bernice had been away. Hardening of the arteries was what they called it. Bernice touched Mrs. Pettaway's shoulder lightly, and her head rose slowly and looked toward the large mirror in front of her. Just then the boy walked in. "Billy, Mr. Brown called to see if you could run the store for him the rest of the afternoon."

Mrs. Pettaway looked at Bernice's reflection in the mirror and said, "Who's that?"

"I was just telling Billy that Mr. Brown wanted him to come run the store for him this afternoon. He's got to take Peggy to the doctor in Vicksburg."

Mrs. Pettaway looked more perplexed than before. "Who's gonna carry me over there?" Bernice glanced at the boy with an amused look. "No ma'am, you just stay right here with me and let me finish fixing your hair. Billy's gonna go over to see Mr. Brown."

The old woman studied her reflection for a long moment and said, "Well, they shot ole Kennedy today, and as bad as everybody talks about Mississippi, what do they do...they done made Paul Johnson the President."

The boy quickly looked at his mother, then back to the old woman and began, "No, Mrs. Pettaway, they made Lyndon Johnson the President, he's..."

The woman continued, "I know Paul Johnson, and he's a good man. He stood in the door up at Ole Miss and dared them to put that nigra in school. Said they'd have to kill him."

Bernice met the boy's gaze and shook her head, almost imperceptibly, "You go on over to the store, he called about thirty minutes ago. And you've still got to dust when you get home. I told you to do it before you went to school."

The boy, careful not to let the screen door slam behind him, walked out into the street as the first drops of rain began to fall on the sidewalk. Big, fat drops that presaged the kind of rain that lays over the Delta for a day or more in the gloom that is November. He crossed the footbridge over Deer Creek as the rain quickened, and barely made the store's double screen doors as the deluge began.

"Bottom's droppin' out, ain't it?" Mr. Brown said from his metal lawn chair as the boy scooted in.

"Yes sir, probably gon' rain the rest of the night. I saw 'em hauling the cotton trailers under the gin shed, they don't ever have enough tarpaulins," he said, pronouncing it "tarpolyins." "That bale's still smokin', maybe the rain will finally put it out."

Mr. Brown looked toward the flyspecked front window. "I don't know, I've seen 'em smolder till after Christmas time. That whole bale'll be rurnt by then. They cain't get the smell out. I bet you Mr. Barrentine's cussin' a blue streak." He stood, looked around the small store, and said, "Go on and make yourself a baloney sandwich or get whatever you want, I got to get going, especially in this rain. We're gon spend the night in Vicksburg. Bailey's comin' in tomorrow morning to open up, and I should be back after dinner, so if you can watch things for a while you can close up about 7." He buttoned his sweater and walked to the side door and said, "Probably won't have too many customers this afternoon with all this rain, but I got my shipment this morning so put some of the stock up if you get a minute." He walked slowly to his car, oblivious to the hammering rain.

Brown's Grocery was a dark, out of the way little place by the railroad track on the edge of the Black section of town known as Bluefront. The haphazard line of houses had gotten its name years before when the owner of the two dozen or so shotgun shacks, plus a converted house juke joint called The Gold Coast, had found a deal on fifty gallons of dark blue paint, leftover as war surplus from Camp Shelby in south Mississippi. The fact that the houses were now painted school bus yellow, ostensibly from some other good deal, made no difference at all to its inhabitants or the people of the town. It was and would forever be Bluefront.

The store's only light came from two flyspecked and greasy windows in the front and four bare lightbulbs hanging from the ceiling. The boy stood in the now quiet store, the rain on the tin roof muffled by the dusty roof beams and the sheer volume of items packed into the little place of business. Shelves loaded with cans, rusted on their bottoms, from years gone by, sacks of flour and meal and sugar, five-gallon buckets of lard, jars of salve, ointments for bleaching skin, patent medicines to cure coughs and fevers, liver problems and stomach aches, tins of Prince Albert and Bugler tobacco, off-brand washing powders and boxes of dry starch, and even a rack of dusty clothes that looked as if no human hand had touched for many years. The truth was that Mr. Brown's only customers were the residents of Bluefront, generally, children sent to the store for the simple necessities of Delta life, and their needs ended at the cold drink boxes filled with Red Rock Cola, Grapette, Diet Rite and the myriad flavors of Barqs drinks, the big glass jars filled with two-for-a-penny cookies, or the glass front meat cooler which held an array of pungent souse, liver cheese, boiled ham, rag bologna, salami, giant jars of pickled eggs and pigs feet, and the huge wheels of what was known locally as "rat cheese." By and large the white residents ignored the store, only a few poor whites who came into town from the country on Saturday afternoon still traded with Mr. Brown, and most of those because they had the same credit arrangement their parents had established years before. They paid off when their cotton was sold in the fall. Throughout the rest of the year they bought on credit, some filling up two long pages in Mr. Brown's big ledger book.

The rain slacked to a steady, insistent peppering. The boy went to the meat cooler and pulled an end hunk of rag bologna out of the chill of the box, put it on the electric meat slicer, cut a healthy, half-inch slice, and laid it on a piece of white butcher paper. He then cut a thick slice of cheese, got a nickel pack of crackers from the shelf, and opened a Barq's root beer. He ate in silence, slumped in the red metal lawn chair. He looked up as the front door opened to see a girl rush inside, shaking the rain from her hair and wiping her face with the sleeve of a thin coat. She stopped when she saw the boy, her arm still held to her forehead. It was Rena. Although he had seen her almost weekly, they had not spoken since the incident in the cotton field some four months before. She met his gaze, straightened her shoulders and marched to the drink box. He started to speak but it was as if his throat had suddenly, and inexplicably, closed and barely managed a ragged, whispered, "Hey," too low for her to hear even if she'd been listening.

He took a long drink from the bottle of root beer, and suddenly aware of the cracker crumbs on his shirt and in his lap, began to brush them onto the floor. He felt the blood rush to his cheeks, and looked in her direction. She lifted the heavy chest-like door of the drink box and stood, motionless, looking down into a forest of bottles in the chilled water. She leaned to reach into the box, but quickly, as if surprised by the iciness of the water, pulled her hand away and stood gazing into the darkness of the drink box. The boy started to stand, to say something, a word or sentence that was not yet formed or considered but instead settled nervously back into the chair. The slow hum of the drink box and cooler motors, the steady rain, and rhythmic swoosh from the cotton compress in the distance framed the moment that was anything but silent. He looked in the direction of the motionless girl. She was crying, and in that moment her shoulders began to shake, gently at first but with increasing strength until her entire body was moving with a force that scared the boy, and a low moan arose from somewhere deep inside the girl that sounded to him plaintive and otherworldly. This time he stood.

He walked to the drink box quietly, watching for a sign or some evidence that she wanted to share her grief or tell him the cause of her disturbing lamentation.

He finally found the courage to ask, "What's wrong, Rena?"

She did not look at him as she whispered, "They kilt him. They just kilt him." "Who killed who?" the boy shot back, puzzled at this pronouncement.

"Didn't they tell y'all? They shot the president today. He's dead." She now looked at the boy, her tears standing in stark contrast to the rain still on her face. In his confusion the boy thought, "Tears look different than rain."

He blurted, "Some people stood up and cheered when they made the announcement over the intercom at school. I know that's wrong, and I'm sorry about the water in the field last summer. I didn't mean..."

The boy stood still. He could smell the faint odor of woodsmoke and bacon grease in her hair and on her body. She turned, the boy now with his arms outstretched toward her, and walked to the screen door, paused without looking back, pushed the door open and walked out into the November rain.

March

It was one of those days when winter seems far past. The air, while not warm, hints of a perfect day, and the ground, while not technically wet, still holds the moisture of the winter rains, and is almost cold. Sock-footed schoolyard children and late afternoon touch football-playing teenagers feel the dampness of winter creep through white crew socks and thin nylon socks like some memory best forgotten. A line of turtles slipped quietly, as if by some prearranged signal or implied order, off the log as the four boys came onto the footbridge over the creek. The creek bank hinted signs of green new growth peeking from the roar of last year's brown and broken Johnson grass and crossvine, and the creek, still swollen from the previous week's rain, ran with uncharacteristic speed to the south. The boys were carrying Red Ryder and Daisy BB guns with the exception of Buddy, who carried a pump action pellet rifle. One carried a brown paper grocery sack filled with Coke bottles and Mason jars.

"Watch before you throw anything down," said Buddy. "Louis Brown told my Daddy that he knew it was us shootin' off the bridge."

The tallest boy dropped the sack on the creosote and tar-covered crossbeams of the bridge, picked out a quart jar and flung it far upstream. "I saw the patrol car at Cecil's. Louis is probably sittin' in the barbershop or the pool hall. He ain't studyin' us. Let's shoot."

And with that, the boys trained their BB guns on the bobbing jar heading toward the bridge. They shot with amazing speed and some degree of accuracy, and within seconds there was a faint, hollow pop, and the jar disappeared under the churning brown water of Deer Creek.

"I hit that sonofabitch!"

"No you didn't, it was me."

"The hell you say, I hit it square on the side. You couldn't hit a gallon jug with that piece of shit."

"Well, throw another one and just you and me'll shoot."

They quickly exhausted the supply of bottles, all the while arguing as to who shot what and who was the best shot and whose BB gun was the truest.

"I bet I can hit that light pole over there," Buddy bragged and took aim at the pole some thirty yards away.

"Do it then, smartass. Hell, that ain't nothin', anybody can hit that."

"See that far streetlight there? I bet I can hit the lightbulb." Buddy pumped the pellet rifle to its maximum and knelt on the bridge, using the handrail to steady the barrel. He took his time, biting the tip of his tongue as if in deep concentration, and finally shot. For a moment they thought he had missed, and made ready to jeer his failure, when the faint but unquestionable sound of the pellet striking the glass globe came to them, and then, seconds later, the undeniable sound of glass shards falling on the street.

"Well, kiss my ass and call me shorty," Billy muttered under his breath. "That was a damn good shot."

"What did I tell you boys? Y'all can call me Dead-Eye Dick from now on."

"I know what we can call you. Mister got-his-ass-in-trouble-again," said the tall boy. "One-way ticket to reform school. Next stop, Parchman." They laughed, but in that nervous and unsettling way when everyone realizes the uncomfortable but irrefutable truth has been spoken.

"Not if they can't catch me. I run better than I shoot." He paused, looking to the far end of the bridge, and said, "Here comes L.C. and Rena. He ain't paid me back that quarter I lent him two damn weeks ago."

"Yeah, he didn't see yo ass or he'd a gone the other way," the tall boy said.

"Don't mess with him, you know he ain't got a penny, if he did he'd have a mouth full of bubble gum," Billy said, looking toward the boy and girl who had stopped when they saw the boys standing on the bridge.

"You got my money, L.C.?" Buddy hollered in their direction. L.C., small for his age, but lean and wiry, grinned at Buddy, looked at his older sister, and turned to run. Buddy dropped the pellet rifle and took off toward the running boy, closing quickly, and, as if in a single motion, pounced on his back like an attacking bear, pinning the other's arms behind his back before crashing to the ground.

"Get offa me! I ain't did nothin' to you."

"Yeah, 'cept not pay me back my money. How 'bout I take it outta yo ass?" Buddy stood up, spun the boy around and put him in a headlock, bending him nearly back to the ground. The other boys had run to the scene of the fight and were looking on in embarrassed silence.

"Let him go, Buddy!" Rena screamed as she ran to her sobbing brother.

Buddy spun the boy around, away from Rena, now twisting and putting more pressure on the boy's neck, and looked at her coldly, quietly. "You better shut your damn mouth. This is between me and L.C."

Rena stopped for a moment, staring at Buddy, stunned in that instant that he wasn't even mad. He was, in fact, mocking and satisfied, almost giddy in his victory. His quarry was overpowered, beaten, dismissed. Rena looked toward the other boys, now shuffling uncomfortably with hands in pockets, staring at the ground, looking everywhere except at the debacle, and rested her gaze on Billy. He was looking toward her, yet not into her face. That she was in his periphery was the most he could gamble, and feeling the heat of her stare, quickly averted his eyes, his cheeks red from the ferment of the fight, or the sudden chill of the now fading afternoon, or the sting of the knowledge that he wouldn't go against Buddy. That he could not go against Buddy. The entire clash had happened in no more than one minute, but the exercise left them spent, even the boys who had nothing to do with the fight.

Rena looked away, then calmly put her hand into the pocket of her dress and drew out a pitiful handful of coins, pennies and nickels and the odd dime. She held them out as an offering, eyes downcast and tear-filled, not in sadness, but with the blunt, distant anger that cannot be salved. "Just let him go," she whispered. "Just let him alone."

Buddy suddenly, and unexpectedly, eased his grip on the boy's neck and let him fall to the ground. He turned to reach for the coins. Wanting, no, seeing the coins slam into his face with the sting of an open-handed slap, to plunge wildly and embed deep into those mocking, hate-filled eyes, rendering them sightless for all time, she hesitated. Her hand clenched as if to make a fist, then relaxed and began to open as her head slowly raised and her still-wet eyes met those she had so recently wanted to hurt. As Buddy reached for the coins, they slipped, as if in slow motion, one by one, onto the cold ground. Buddy dropped to his knees and scrambled for his meager repayment, the score settled.

"Come on L.C." Rena helped her brother to his feet, brushing the brown grass and leaf bits from his face and hair, a dark stain of water spreading from the knees of his jeans, his shirt torn and in disarray. Rena placed her hand lightly on his neck as they turned to walk across the footbridge and on home.

Shirley's Gone

Shirley Stewart and me, 2014

After I bought the house, I would run into Shirley at the grocery store or at Chuck's Dairy Bar, the local eatery. We talked a lot. She had married, had children, and worked at the school for many years. She had lived a good life. One night when I was invited to give a talk at the Rolling Fork Library, I was happy to see Shirley in the audience. I told part of this story to the gathered crowd, and everyone got a big laugh when I told of her slapping me down in the cotton field. I asked Shirley to stand up, and she laughed and said, "You better watch out, Willy Bearden, I'll slap you down again!" That brought the house down.

Shirley died of cancer in 2015. I don't know why I never shared this story with her, though I know she would have liked it. I was a little afraid the fictionalized parts might make her sad somehow. It's funny how we are tied to people, inescapably, across the bonds of time and explanation. I have a feeling I'll see Shirley again.

The Girls Reminded Me

The girls and a couple of guys. L to R, Izzy, Fern, Marilyn, Willy, Rae Nell, George, Jean, and Ann.

I went to school with this group of girls who, even though many of them live in different parts of the country now, are still in close contact and even take a group trip together each year. I am envious of their closeness and their natural defense and support of one another. During the last fifty years or so all the girls have been there for one another through marriages and divorces, births and deaths. There is an unbroken thread that runs through their lives, beginning with birthday parties and kindergarten. Now, as they approach old age, the lines are intact and strong as ever. I envy that closeness, and wish I had it with my old friends, but it seems that too much time has passed, and we were left in the middle to work out our own stories, our own paths, without the day-to-day help from one another. I had dinner with three of them a couple of years ago, and I was so touched by how much they remembered, and really treasured those times we had together. They are a big part of my story.

"Remember in the seventh grade when you would take over the class on Mondays to tell us what you had done over the weekend? Poor Miss Moody left in tears and never came back after the Thanksgiving break. We all knew you were going to be famous. Remember what the class prophecy said about you? Johnny Carson's replacement."

I joined their class in 1963, when they were twelve and I was thirteen. I had failed the seventh grade, and as my class moved on to the eighth grade, I repeated. This was possibly the most embarrassing thing I had ever done in my life, walking into that seventh grade classroom on the first day of school, finding a desk amongst those kids who had always been in the class below me. I took a seat on the second row by the window and watched as Coach Cain came into class and laid a dime on the edge of his desk. "This is my dime," he said. "If I come back here on this day next year, I want to see my dime right here on the desk. That's about as simple as I can make it folks. You are about to enter into adulthood now, and the most important lesson I can teach you is to be honest as the day is long. That would about get it, now wouldn't it?" Thirty heads nodded. "We've got a new person here in class with us. You all know Willy." My face burned with embarrassment and I thought for a minute I might throw up. "I'm going to ask him to be my assistant as you get used to changing classrooms and all the new things that you'll learn in junior high school. He will be here to answer any questions you might have and to help you through the next few weeks. If I'm not in the classroom for any reason, Willy is in charge and I expect you to respect him just as you would me." Coach Cain. Probably the finest man God ever put on this earth. He knew what I was going through, and he turned it around so I wouldn't lose face, so I felt important. I visited Coach Cain several times throughout the years, and I always thanked him for making my second transition into the seventh grade an easy one. He spared me the embarrassment and humiliation that I was so sure was coming. I don't cry about much, but I just cried as I wrote that. This one story points to the kindness that people have shown me throughout my life.

That was the year I joined the girls' class. The same year as my father had spent the month of January in the state mental hospital at Whitfield after having gone crazy and running through the streets of Rolling Fork with a baseball bat screaming at people who weren't there.

After that I had several episodes of what I can only describe as fugue states, where I would kind of blank out in class, sounds would become ultra distinct, light would fade, and I would become aware of my own breathing and my aloneness in a world filled with people. I have never told anyone about these episodes for fear they might diagnose me with something awful. Anyway, they gradually went away, and by the time I was about fourteen they never returned. This feeling haunts me, or maybe that's too strong a word. It concerns me and appears in my mind far too frequently, that there must be another reality hidden between or amongst wakefulness and sleep, dark and light. It has to be there because I see or remember flashes of it every now and again, talking with someone, driving on a long stretch of highway, waking from a long sleep, that the boundaries, the edges, that slice of neither, that thickness of a human hair must contain its own plane of existence or reality, because I feel in a significant, profound way, the hidden truthfulness of it. I wonder if my glimpses of or exposure to this thing, began when I was sitting in class when gradually everything would begin to go away from me, to retreat from the moment and become a faint, tinny, echoey tether to that side of reality while the new thing tried to emerge. And the new thing, the separate reality never quite came through, so I don't know what I missed. But every time this has happened I have felt an incredible exhaustion when it finally passed, a ringing sensation in my body like when you're a kid and you run, headlong, into something like a tree or a wall, or somebody tackles you really hard and your whole body hums and pulsates with something beyond pain.

This is the trauma that hangs around.

The Red Counts

The Red Counts was a dance band from Jackson, Mississippi. They were the second live band I ever heard. The first was a group I never actually saw, only listened to while standing at the back of the Gold Coast, a notorious Black juke joint at the end of the street behind our house in Rolling Fork. I was about five and slipped off to see where the thumping sound was coming from. I walked through the dusty Johnson grass to the back of the converted house and stood there, my arms reaching out to touch the vibrating building as the band practiced on a hot summer afternoon. I don't know what they were playing, but I knew I wanted more. More of that feeling. More of that driving thud that pulsed through my little boy body. I had listened to the radio and records as long as I could remember, but this was something completely different. I could actually feel this music. I knew instinctively that I couldn't go into the Gold Coast, though nothing would have happened to me if I had, but I wanted to see who these people were and what their instruments looked like, and how they looked while they were playing.

My oldest brother, Gaines, was a freshman at Hinds Junior College in Raymond, Mississippi in 1960, and he became friends with some of the guys in the Red Counts. Before long they were booked to play the Junior/Senior Prom in the gymnasium in Rolling Fork. This was typically one of the biggest events of the year in our little town.

In the weeks leading up to the dance, I pestered my mother as to whether the band was going to stop by our house before the dance. There had been some talk of them eating supper with us. I was ten then and certified crazy about music, having listened incessantly to my brother's stack of records (of course, when he wasn't around) that included Fats Domino, Little Richard, Elvis Presley, The Bill Black Combo, Carl Perkins, Mose Allison, and a smattering of Peter, Paul and Mary, The Rooftop Singers and Pete Seeger. It was an eclectic collection, and before long I knew every lyric to every cut. I didn't know what I was going to do in life, but it was going to be something connected to the feeling I got when I listened to those records.

I had saved for a guitar some months before, and when the box arrived from Spiegel, I could hardly keep from crying. My own guitar, a short-scale plywood, sunburst-painted little guitar that sounded like a slice of heaven to me. Not knowing how to tune it, I spent the first few weeks just holding it in my lap, strumming lightly on the out-of-tune strings, dreaming about the day I could play a song all the way through. Mainly, I fantasized about playing in a real band.

I don't know if it had anything to do with reality or divine intervention, but my prayers were answered when my brother called and said the band would be stopping by our house for supper before the prom. I began scheming. I had to maneuver some way to get myself into that gym. I was not going to let this once-in-a-lifetime moment find me sitting in my living room watching "The Lawrence Welk Show" with my mother. But how to get past the teachers and the principal, much less talk my mother into letting me out of the house? There had to be a way. I ran every scenario my ten-year-old brain could imagine, but everything seemed silly and destined to fail. I still hadn't figured out what I was going to do when the long black Cadillac pulled up in front of our house. I had been sitting on the front steps since I got home from school, just to make sure I didn't somehow miss them. I don't think I had ever been that apprehensive. The Cadillac pulled up, the window rolled down and a guy in shades with a cigarette hanging from his mouth looked at me and said, "Anybody named Willy around here?" I was stunned. I couldn't speak. I never felt so cool in my life. This cat had spoken my name.

The band's guitar player was a guy named Jerry Puckett, and his pompadour, shades, and the cigarette spoke volumes to me. He and the rest of them piled out of the car and walked into our little cracker box of a house. I remember suddenly feeling embarrassed about the big water stains on the wallpaper on the living room ceiling. As I walked in with them, everything in our house looked shabby in a way I had never before noticed. They didn't seem to mind and came right in and laid into the hamburgers and hotdogs my mother had fixed. I still hadn't said a word, but I was watching every move they made. They were dressed for the prom in their regular outfits: red tuxedo coats with black trim, black pants with a satin strip down the leg, and, of course, cool shoes all around. I figured that Jerry was the leader, so I looked at him and said, "Can I go?"

He smiled and said, "Go where?"

"To the dance. Can I go with y'all to the dance? I promise I won't do anything but just sit there and listen." My brother glared at me.

"I don't know if any other kids are going to be there. What do you think the teachers would say?" He said in a way that told me he really didn't care what the teachers thought.

One of the other guys piped up and said, "We could put him in the bass drum case and sneak him in." They all laughed. I saw my opening.

"Mama, can I go? I won't stay long (lie). I promise I'll walk home after just a little while (lie)." The truth is we lived just across the street from the school. She said to the group, "Well, if he promises not to get in your way, and if you promise to send him home if he does, then he can go."

And just like that, I was going to the dance. And not just going to the dance, I was going with the band! I kind of fancied myself as a junior member of the Red Counts.

We got to the gym, and they made me curl up inside the big bass drum case, and before I knew it I was sitting on a lunchroom stool behind the drum riser. I could see around the drummer and watch the other guys in the band, and the high school kids dancing in front of them. For the next three hours I sat, transfixed, as they did songs by Ray Charles, Elvis, the Bill Black Combo, Little Richard, and even Pat Boone. During the evening, a couple of the teacher chaperones gave me the side-eye, but no one said anything about me being there. I walked out of the gym at midnight and helped the band pack up their instruments and amps and watched them drive off toward Highway 61 and back to Jackson. I remember thinking that they had a long way to go before they could go to sleep. I was suddenly more tired than I had ever been.

Everything was so quiet as I walked across the dew-wet grass of the schoolyard, the place where we played "pop the whip" and "dodgeball" at recess every day. It would somehow never look the same to me.

Our porch light was on, but the rest of the house was dark as I quietly walked into the pool of light from the bare bulb of the streetlight at the end of our street. I took my shoes off and tiptoed to my bedroom. I stood, looking out the window toward the school grounds. The house was so quiet. I laid down with my clothes still on and fell into a deep and satisfying sleep. I had found my people.

Church Camp

In the summer of 1963, I went to two church camps. In early June, they loaded us in cars and we made the five-hour drive to Pass Christian, Mississippi, on the Gulf of Mexico. Our counselor was Allan. He was a football star at Mississippi College. We were so in awe of him, it was like being in the presence of Elvis Presley or something. I still remember how he would stand there in the mornings looking in the mirror and put that pink Butch Wax on the front of his flat-top, combing it with so much attention to detail that we kids just looked at each other with knowing nods. He was a good kid. I say kid because he couldn't have been more than nineteen or twenty at the time. In our Bible study sessions in the cabin at night, he would talk about what Jesus meant to him. He said Jesus was his best friend, the person he could tell any and everything, and the person he could ask for forgiveness when he needed it. It was an inspiring week, though I now remember that we didn't have any coed activities except meals and the nightly revival service. Anyway, one night at the revival they made us all get up right in the middle of Brother Reese's sermon, walk to the Olympic-sized swimming pool, and gather around as they handed each child a paper plate with a little birthday cake candle stuck in the middle. They lit the candles and instructed us to place the plates in the water and give them a push toward the middle of the pool. Brother Reese was really cranked up at this point, preaching hellfire and damnation, when he screamed, "You don't know what's going to happen to you in your life! You don't even know what's going to happen in the next five minutes! Your life is like that candle yonder, and it could go out at any minute." Just then, as I was watching my plate and candle mingle with the other two hundred or so, it went out. Just as simple as that. It went out. I froze in panic, wondering if I could have been watching the wrong candle, but I knew I hadn't. I started to speak out, to tell someone that my candle had gone out, but I stayed quiet, staring at the little wisp of smoke that arose from my life, and something came over me like a warm blanket on that hot June night in Mississippi. I knew that I would be all right. I knew that none of that mattered. I reckoned that I didn't need to listen to Brother Reese anymore, or even Allan. I wasn't rebellious or in any way trying to convince the other boys to be rebels. I was just comfortable in not knowing. God couldn't be as random and cruel as all that. Not to children especially. If he was, I didn't want to have anything to do with him.

Two weeks after that, we went to Camp Bratton-Green, the Episcopal camp, where we did everything coed. They seemed to understand that boys and girls needed to learn how to act with one another. Archery, swimming, crafts, hiking, and there I fell in love with a little brown-haired girl who wore a turned-down sailor hat. They even had a dance every night after supper and played songs from the best stocked jukebox I had ever heard. The girl, Tina, and I were best buddies, holding hands when we walked out to the dance floor, twisting to Chubby Checker, and singing along with Del Shannon's falsetto on "Runaway." It was the most rewarding and relaxing time I may have ever had. I decided that although I would probably have to keep going to the Baptist church, I was, at heart, an Episcopalian. My father's family were all Episcopalians, although he might have gone to church once every five years. There was an unspoken caste system in the Delta, a system that looked primarily at church affiliation to determine one's standing in the community. Although the Episcopalians had lost influence to the Snopes-ish Baptists, there remained an understanding that Episcopalians were somehow better.

I just Googled Allan and found that he was, indeed, the pastor of a mega Baptist church in Texas, though he had left his last church under a cloud of financial improprieties. I found a picture of him and although he didn't have the flattop, he had what would pass today for it, that newsman helmet haircut. I wonder what the story was.

The Governor's Chair

When I am introduced to a crowd at a speaking engagement, I am reminded in a flash of memory of Coach Mullins. He was our school principal in Rolling Fork. One day, during my senior year, he called me out in the crowded hallway and said, "Willy Bearden, if you keep running your mouth, you'll never amount to anything." That stung, but he and I never had a good relationship anyway. I had been on the receiving end of some of his brutal paddlings, and I was looking forward to graduating and never having to deal with him again. I always thought he believed I was the instigator of an unfortunate incident that happened when we were in the ninth grade and went on a field trip to the Mississippi State capitol in Jackson, where my friend, Robert, pooted in the governor's chair.

While there is always the risk that a person engaged in this kind of non-controversial folksy history, semi-funny, softball humor could begin to take themselves seriously (and quickly become unbearable to those around him), I have approached the activity with a great deal of self-deprecation and un-full-of-shitness. These are what my wife calls my "Dr. Bearden" moments, where a hundred or so audience members look upon me as I am introduced, and later one of them invariably refers to me as Dr. Bearden. I always get a chuckle out of it. My super power is to always remember that I'm a 14-year-old idiot at heart.

Anyway, back to Robert. He was one of my best friends and was standing right beside me in line. We had ridden the yellow school bus from Rolling Fork to Jackson, and gone to Governor John Bell Williams' office in the Capitol building. The famous one-armed former congressman set about making a big deal of each of us getting to sit in his chair for a few seconds, and how we could forever say that we were the governor for a brief time. I saw the look on Robert's face, a look of bemused contempt. I knew instinctively there would be trouble. Rob whispered to me, "I'm gonna poot in the governor's chair."

I froze. I whispered frantically, "No, don't do that, please. We're all gonna get in trouble if you do that." I was in a panic, because I knew he absolutely would do something like that, and I was standing right beside him and would thus be implicated.

"It's my destiny," he said solemnly. That was one of his favorite things to say. Then he smiled his knowing smile that I'd seen so many times when things were about to go south.

"Please," I whispered, "I'm begging you, don't do it."

He just smiled at me. Sure enough, when it was his time to sit in the chair, he blew one out. It sounded like a duck quacking or a chair leg scraping across the floor. The teachers were mortified, but the governor looked like he wanted to laugh. The rest of the visit was a hot blur in my mind. We got sent to the principal's office as soon as we got off the school bus back to school, and among other punishments, that night I had to tell my mother.

"He did what?" she said, completely bewildered.

"He pooted in the governor's chair," I said softly, like it was a normal thing to say.

"He what? And, I don't like that word, it sounds nasty."

"You know... he... tooted in the Governor's chair."

"Why in the world would he do something like that? That's awful. Passing wind, and right there in front of everybody? Who all was there? You didn't dare him to do that, did you?"

"No, I begged him not to do it."

She just shook her head. "Is he right upstairs?"

"I don't know. He said it was his destiny."

"His what?"

"His destiny."

"That boy..." she sighed. "Country come to town. Lord have mercy, we can't take y'all anywhere. His destiny, my foot." She said this last bit as she walked into the kitchen. For the next few days I would catch her looking at me hard, like I was from another planet. These many years later I look back at this incident with great relish, and not a little pride, at knowing Robert for so many years. He died in 2018 after his cancer came back. He was 66 years old. We had played music together since we were kids, laughed more than most people ever dream of, and shared experiences that only a precious few get to live. He truly was one of the most intelligent and insightful people I've ever known. Hardly a day goes by that I don't quote him or relate a story to someone who needs to hear it. He was a free spirit, and didn't give a flying fuck what anyone thought about him. His death hit me hard. The last time I saw him was a couple of weeks before he died, and he looked at me with a smile and tears in his eyes, knowing this was the last time we'd be together. He died on October 1, 2018. A little bit of me died that day, too. But, if I ever get the chance to sit in a governor's chair, you can be pretty sure what's going to happen.

The Ditch

My writing room, Rolling Fork, Mississippi, 2012

I woke early this morning, my sleep plagued with a memory that wouldn't come to the surface. I had driven down from Memphis to my house in Rolling Fork the day before. I had plans to finish a couple of editing projects and do some writing over the next four or five days. This time, my first night in the house was restless. I tossed and turned, and didn't get much sleep. Though I knew I would fall into the habit of my refuge and get a lot of work done after the first day, I woke with a sense of unease, and I questioned why I had even come.

I took a walk outside just after sunrise, and walking along the road in back of the house, I stopped by the ditch, a thing that was part of the makeshift system they employed to move water out of the town after the '27 flood, now all round-shouldered and shallow where it used to be deep and sharply defined. The ditch. And then it came to me. A gray day in early March, I don't remember what year, but it was pouring rain outside, and I was in the house when the phone rang. A neighbor lady, one of the rich ladies in town, called to say that Daddy's car had run up into her yard during the rainstorm and she was worried that he might be hurt. I ran the block or so to her house, and there was his car, against a tree in her side yard. I went to the window and he was sitting there with blood running from his nose, an open pint of Early Times between his legs. "You alright?" I yelled in the driving rain as he rolled the window down.

"Yeah, I think I'm out of gas. The goddam car won't crank," he slurred.

"Daddy, you hit Mrs. Tansey's tree. She called me."

"Here, help me get out." He stumbled out into the rain, pint in hand, and began staggering around the car.

"That damn car's out of gas."

"Daddy, we better go home. Come on, we can get the car in a little bit."

"Alright, I'll get Cecil to bring some goddam gas and get it cranked."

We began walking the short distance to our house, him sidewheeling along, me trying to help him stay on his feet. He kept trying to take a drink from the pint as he walked, but mostly he was missing his mouth and spilling it down his already-soaked shirt. The blood had been quickly washed from his face. We had made it around to our street when he veered wide and stepped into the ditch, which by this point was rushing with rainwater. It was truly one of those slow motion moments. He kind of slid down the side of the ditch on one foot and sat down slowly, the water coming up almost to his shoulders. He started to laugh and tried to reach for me, but then got this look of absolute fear in his eyes. I watched as the pint bottle floated away from where he was sitting, the amber bourbon still sloshing against the sides. It was like I could see every drop of rain as it fell before my eyes, and through those drops sat the person I loved and despised, reaching out for me to help him out of the rushing water. I stood there. He tried to reach for the side of the ditch, but that put him off balance and he fell forward, his head going under for the first time. His arms were flailing as he came up sputtering and yelling something. I moved a step closer to the side of the ditch and then stopped. "Hey, here! Get my hand!" As soon as he reached toward me he went down again. This time his body tumbled, in slow motion, about six feet down the ditch. I walked along watching. I looked around to see if anyone had seen us, but the rain was pounding so heavily it would have been hard to distinguish anything more than a short distance away. I stood there as he tried to right himself. Then, as if by magic, there appeared beside me a huffing, puffing figure in a yellow raincoat. It was Mr. Alvin, a man who lived on the street behind us. He looked at me, and then jumped into the water and pulled Daddy out by his jacket collar. Daddy's legs were kicking violently when he came out of the water, and within a second or two he was on his feet.

"Damn, Alvin, let go of me!"

"Son, you were bobbin' like a cork on a cane fishing pole. You better be glad this boy was here to save you. If I hadn't heard him yellin' you woulda' been in some serious trouble," he laughed nervously.

Yelling? Was I yelling? I have no memory of that. In my mind, I think I was ready to let him drown. Let there be a tragic, final, end to this, but something automatic must have taken over and caused me to yell. I was instantly ashamed of myself for wanting him to die.

"Whew, that scared the shit out of me, Norman. Here, let me help you home."

"No, I'm alright," he looked to me and asked, "Where's my pint?"

"It floated away when you fell in," I said.

"Well, goddam!"

Mr. Alvin turned to me. "Can you get him home?"

"Yessir."

"Well, don't let him out in this mess. It's raining like a cow pissin' on a flat rock. Y'all go on now."

We walked home, him staggering.

"We'll go get the car tomorrow." I said.

My Mojave

Albuquerque, NM, 1972. Photo by Gaines Bearden

My brother died two weeks ago. He had just turned 80 and was living in a group residence in Denver for people living with and dying of Alzheimer's disease. I hadn't talked to him in three years or so. The last time was on his birthday in December 2018. That day, he seemed to remember me, in fact, his voice went up an octave and I could tell he was so pleased to say my name. "Willy!"

We talked for a few minutes, mainly with me asking very simple questions like, "Did you take a drive and see the aspens turning this year?" and him asking his wife if they did. It was a pleasant conversation, though I could tell he was confused for much of it. When we said goodbye I knew I would never hear his voice again.

Gaines was nine years older than me. He was born on December 5, 1941, just two days before the Japanese attacked Pearl Harbor, and started the U.S. version of World War II. He couldn't have had a more inauspicious beginning. My mother had traveled home to rural Leake County, Mississippi, the community of Standing Pine to be precise, from Port Gibson, a journey of 115 miles, where she was working as a first-year beautician, or beauty operator, as they called it back then. I can't imagine how long that trip had taken. The winter roads in Mississippi were atrocious, at best.

She had come home to stay with her parents, for a reason none of us ever knew, and had a tiny, three-pound baby in the house where she herself had been born. She had turned twenty that summer. I once heard her talking to a friend, Peggy Wilson, a woman who came over in the afternoon once or twice a week to have coffee, and she said when my brother was born he didn't have eyelashes. I was five or six at the time, and I remember studying my older brother's eyelashes for years after that. How frightening it must have been to have a premature baby at that time, and the world turn completely crazy two days later. That war was the most disruptive event of the twentieth century, and coming on the heels of the Great Depression, it must have seemed like the world was ending.

Three years later, the war was to take my mother and brother to Newport, Rhode Island, where my father was a projectionist at the Navy training school. There are a few photographs of my mother and brother standing in the snow outside a small house, my brother astride a cannon in a park, my mother and her new friends having a picnic on a beach somewhere. Her time there was marked by letters from her mother and sisters, and the death of her brother, an Army sergeant who was killed in Holland on March 23, 1945.

Later in life, she said she'd always wanted to go back to Rhode Island. As different as it was, and as strange as the people were, there was something about it that suited her. My brother only remembered what the photographs bore witness to, and the faint memory of little boys playing in the snow.

I was eight when my brother graduated from Rolling Fork High School. That was 1959. I have very little memory of him living in the house with us, but after he left home and did his six months on active duty in the National Guard, his visits took on a grand significance. He was always coming and going, telling stories of the fools he served with in the Guard, or the people he had met at Hinds Junior College, or of hitchhiking to and from school, or bringing records into the house and treating us to folk music or jazz. He quickly became my idol.

A year or two later, at Delta State College, he started a folk singing group that played around the Delta. He carried a Yamaha nylon string guitar with him everywhere. He taught many of my friends how to make chords and how to play specific songs. I was in heaven. There were records by Pete Seeger, the Kingston Trio, Peter, Paul and Mary, the Rooftop Singers, and Mose Allison. This was exactly what my twelve-year-old self needed. When I was around him, I watched his every move. I wanted to be just like Gaines. Even more than that, I wanted to live his life. I pored over his college yearbooks and can still remember the names of his classmates. He seemed to know and like lots of the Italian kids from Greenville and Leland and Shaw. Surnames like Fioranelli, Cassia, Pietro, and Fratesi dotted the autograph pages of his Delta State yearbooks. I began to understand that we had a rich mix of ethnicities as our neighbors. Jewish people, Syrians, Lebanese, Greeks, and Chinese, all populating this postage stamp of land called the Mississippi Delta.

On the hot summer afternoons when he was away from the house working, I began to listen intently to the lyrics, and I began to change. Maybe I was just growing up, but I heard things in those songs that made me question so much that was going on in my town, my state, and my country. I had never heard the term "social change" but in my heart, I knew I was hearing the truth. I began to believe that if everyone could listen to these songs, change would be inevitable. I wondered why they didn't feature these songs in our church. Surely, this is exactly what Jesus was teaching nineteen hundred years ago, but those who crowded the Rolling Fork First Baptist Church on Sunday mornings and Wednesday nights were the same people who gave money and support to the White Citizens' Council, the same who paid slave wages to the Black people who worked for them in their homes, on their farms, and in their stores. These were the same people who thought Italians, Lebanese, and Greeks were cut from the same cloth as Blacks, and therefore weren't really "white people." World War II had signaled a change in that attitude, and by the 1970s these folks had been welcomed into the club, as it were.

By the time I was thirteen, I had little use for church. I still feel that way today. I just watched a documentary on Fannie Lou Hamer, a woman who lived up the road in Ruleville, and was a force in the civil and voting rights struggle of the 1960s in Mississippi. I don't know how many times she was beaten, or how many times she got thrown in jail on trumped-up charges, but I was awestruck by how she possessed more clarity, enlightenment, and grace than all her tormentors combined.

So, any time my brother left the house, I would listen to those records, hour after hour, and I began to pick up the symbolism in the folk songs. It was truly one of the first things I ever completely understood. These people, these singers and songwriters, who weren't from around here, had seen something going on, something with the deepest of roots, the most elemental of what might be called human goodness, and they shared it with all who would listen. Across the country, the crowd was growing.

There was a lot at stake in the Mississippi Delta. The forces behind the status quo were many and powerful. The fear that Black people would one day simply not show up in the cotton fields to chop the johnson grass, or not show up in the kitchens to cook the family meals, wash the clothes, drive the tractors, raise the kids, or do the multitudinous dirty work that white people wouldn't do, was very real, and, surprisingly, tempered a lot of what went on in the Delta. There was a fine line between the intimidation and retribution that Black folks endured. The fact of the Delta was that the population in the mid-60s was over 60% African American. Many counties had Black populations of over 70%. Any change in the regular program was feared to be disastrous.

I remember the almost daily assaults from the boys at the barbershop and Sundays from the pulpit on the beatniks and COFO workers who had invaded our Eden, which made me admire them even more. And don't wake up the Beatles. The same people who were sounding the alarm bells when Elvis shook his hips and the girls fell out were now convinced the Beatles were going to be the end of civilization. I became strangely enamored with those brave souls who left their college towns in Michigan and Ohio and Wisconsin and other far-flung places to spend the hot summer in a tumble-down shack on the edge of a cotton field in Issaquena County, Mississippi, teaching children and adults alike how to read and write, and ultimately, how to register to vote. Whether they knew the very real danger they were in, I'll never know, but something I saw when I was working for the Mansours at the Blue and Gold Grocery in Rolling Fork still is as present in my mind as it was on that day in July of 1964.

The Mansours were Lebanese immigrants who set up shop in Rolling Fork in the 1940s, first running a pool hall and a small cafe, and later opening a full-sized grocery store where they catered to a mostly country clientele of poor whites and poorer Blacks who came into the store on Saturday nights after having spent the afternoon at the picture show or browsing through the five and dime store. I was a stock boy and a sacker. I must've carried out tons of neck bones, fifty-pound sacks of flour, and buckets of lard to dusty cars full of children and old people, tired from their day in town. Saturday nights would find us at the store till after 11 PM, mopping the long aisles, and sweeping the littered parking lot.

On the long summer afternoons, I'd slip off to the big cooler and open a quart of chocolate milk. I'd take a long drink of the thick, sweet Grenada Farms chocolate milk, and stand in front of the blower for as long as I dared, knowing that Mr. Mansour would be watching to make sure I wasn't loafing. He was a grouchy old man who was constantly on my ass about something, but I knew that as bad as he was, I wasn't standing out in a cotton field with a hoe in my hand. I never thought to ask why the Mansours had left Syria or Lebanon and come to little Rolling Fork. Maybe the war displaced them as it did so many others. I would love to have sat down with him and heard the details of his journey. In a different time, we might have been friends, but my main occupation at thirteen was staying out of his way. My brother Jeff worked at the store from the time he was twelve till he was in college. That job bought him a moped, a stereo, a great record collection, clothes, and a Ducati motorcycle. I never seemed to hang on to the money I made, instead frittering it away at the pool hall or in the many jukeboxes around town. I had a love/hate relationship with the store and Mr. Mansour. I was good for about three months, then I simply couldn't stand it anymore, and I'd quit. A few months would pass and Jeff would say something like, "Mr. Mansour wants to know if you can work this Saturday," and I'd be stuck there for another three or four months.

One afternoon, one of the student COFO workers came into the store with a couple of Black teenagers. They were wandering the aisles, obviously enjoying the air conditioning, when a man, a known KKK member, I'll call him Mr. Fant, walked into the store. I knew something was about to blow. Old man Fant saw the COFO worker and immediately flew into a rage, chasing the young man around the store in what I can only describe as a bizarre, almost cartoon moment. The whole thing couldn't have lasted more than twenty or thirty seconds, and when the kid hit the front door, he was in full sprint mode, and Fant was hot on his tail. They ran down the street and out of sight. I know Fant didn't catch him because the boy would have been beaten half to death. I watched out the window as Fant huffed and puffed back to the store parking lot and drove away in his pickup. Mr. Mansour told me to get back to work and to not tell anyone what had happened. That would have been bad for business. The young man never darkened the door of our grocery store again, but I saw him a couple of weeks later, getting out of a car in front of the high school. A couple of months after that, Thelma Horton, a Black girl from Mayersville was to join the tenth-grade class at Rolling Fork High School and begin her own time in hell for the next three years.

I still think about the young man to this day. He was but one of the many who came and served their fellow human beings in the Mississippi Delta that summer long ago. He would be an old man now, nearing eighty. I wonder if he ever feels old man Fant huffing and puffing behind him on a hot June day in 1964.

And in a heartbreaking remnant of irony that seemed to create some bizarre and tragic sense of symmetry, Mr. Fant's boy, Claude, was killed in Vietnam in 1966. I wonder if it ever occurred to the old man that his son was seen as an interloper in someone else's country, fighting, and literally laying down his life for the rights of an oppressed brown people. Claude was 22 years old and never combed gray hair

My friend Carl and I played and sang Simon and Garfunkel's 'He Was My Brother' at the Rolling Fork Jaycees' annual dinner in April of 1969. We were seniors then, and I was so done with Rolling Fork. I was ready to leave and never come back. As I looked out over the audience, I could see the disgust on their faces as they listened to the words about the three civil rights workers who were killed in Philadelphia, Mississippi in 1964.

He was my brother
Five years older than I
He was my brother
Twenty three years old the day he died...

The song was an indictment of our way of life, the things we accepted and the things we never reconciled though we had the opportunity every day of our lives to begin to set things straight. Those lyrics had been in my ears and in my mind for a couple of years now, and I had to say them out loud.

After that, Bill the Barber wouldn't cut my hair. That was okay with me, but I had to plan accordingly to hit the other barber shop before about 3 pm because Clyde nipped all through each morning at that pint of Old Crow he kept in the little room behind the shoeshine stand. I made the mistake of going there late one Saturday afternoon and wound up with the back of my hair skinned up three inches above my collar. It took a while for that to grow out.

***

Carl's daddy, Buddy, was murdered on a Saturday night in 1968 when he walked into his aging parents' house after getting a phone call that his brother, Huey, was tearing up the house and threatening his parents with a butcher knife. It seemed that Huey was hiding behind the front door and plunged the butcher knife into Buddy's heart as soon as he walked through the door. They said he was dead before he hit the floor. For years after, Carl would stare off in the distance and say, "The day he gets out of Parchman, I'm going to kill him." I knew he meant it, and I never believed a jury in Rolling Fork would have convicted him. That was one of the perks of living in a small town back then. He may have done some time, though not in Parchman, and he would be able to come and go from the jailhouse pretty much as he pleased. They would have him mowing the creek bank and washing the sheriff's car, but he would have never missed a Thanksgiving or Christmas dinner at his mama's table.

Carl and I were close then. When I hitchhiked into Memphis in late December of 1971, it was in his house where I laid my sleeping bag on the floor that first night. He was living on Alcy Road, just off Bellevue Blvd. in a rough neighborhood with a group of Vietnam vets and some other hangers-on who were completely out of control. They were heroin addicts, and, by extension, burglars, car and motorcycle thieves, and weren't afraid of anything or anyone. Or maybe the opposite is true, they were afraid of everything and everyone. They had survived the chaos of Vietnam only to be tossed out of the one place they thought they could count on for money, a bed and food, drugs, and a little direction. They stole my stereo system the first week I lived with them and were unapologetic and very matter-of-fact when I confronted them. They told me something like, "The world's a tough place, kid. You better get tough with it," all the while concocting another fix. They all carried pistols, and were constantly laughing about shooting somebody in the "fuckin' face." I was scared out of my mind for the entire two weeks I stayed there. I witnessed one of them die one night, only to be slapped back into life a few moments later.

Although he's been gone eight or ten years now, having had a heart attack after mowing the lawn one Saturday afternoon, I still think of Carl and the times we had. Our lives went in separate directions after he moved to Jackson, Mississippi, in 1974, a move he desperately needed. He told me as he was leaving that he had "worn Memphis out," but I knew it was the other way around. We called those early Memphis times the "mad dog days." As was the case with a lot of young people back then, we were always trying to be the weirdest of the weird. It was a time of great change, with kids questioning their government, their parents, religion, the way they looked and dressed, everything. To be seen as ordinary was a sin of the greatest magnitude. The funny thing is the vast majority of these hippie freaks were voting for Ronald Reagan by the time they were in their early thirties.

Early in 1972, this lady rented us a duplex on a Memphis street called Dawnwood Cove, off Ketchum Road in the old Frisco/Charjean neighborhood. It was a mishmash of crackerbox houses from just after WWII, a new, sprawling apartment complex nestled next to the new Interstate 240 southern loop, and several odd streets of handmade houses from the 1920s, when the Frisco railroad expanded the yards under the viaduct over Airways Blvd. The airport buyout was a hot topic, and money appeared to buy out much of the neighborhood along the flight path to the Memphis airport. The smart among our neighbors took the money and ran, and those who held on for whatever reason were left to hobble along for several years with the sky filling with louder and louder jets taking off and landing in a non-stop nightmare of noise and jet fuel mist released over the neighborhood.

We quickly had seven people living in the two-bedroom, one-bath place. Our other-side-of-the-wall neighbor was a cute girl from Clarksdale who we drove completely crazy with our loud nightly parties and constant blaring music. We were a strange crew of junior college dropouts from the Delta, with a few lost girls and various misfits rounding out our ragged family.

In the summer of 1972, Carl and I quit our jobs at the liquor warehouse and got a ride with a friend who was just back from Vietnam and headed to Fort Huachuca in southern Arizona. He took us to El Paso, where we stayed with my aunt and spent a few days wandering around Juarez, Mexico's dusty, pulsing streets. We hit the road and hitchhiked to Albuquerque, where my brother Gaines lived. We spent a few days with him, hiking the crest of Sandia Peak, riding the city bus downtown every day, cooking hamburgers on the grill in the late afternoons, laughing, and watching my niece and nephew play in their wading pools.

On the day we left, my brother took us to a freeway entrance and we sat in his Ford station wagon for a few minutes. I knew he was nervous that we were heading north to Denver, and then back across Kansas, Oklahoma, and Arkansas to get back to Memphis. He took a picture of us standing by the interstate sign, our backpacks loaded with a little food, dirty clothes, and some cheap junk we'd bought in Juarez. We walked up the long entrance ramp, and when I looked back he was still sitting there. I often wondered if he wanted to go with us on our adventure. Maybe he was just worried about me. He was always wound a little tighter than me, and I sensed that my life during these vagabond days made him uncomfortable.

In the years after, whenever I talked to him about the civil rights movement or the war in Vietnam, he had more and more excuses to offer and reasons why I wasn't seeing and understanding the whole picture. I finally just dropped it, but I kept wondering if this was to be my fate. I couldn't imagine changing my belief system, but all around me were people I knew and respected who were having second thoughts about the very things I assumed we all held sacred. I have been accused of being naive and I have suffered misjudgments and mistakes. In the end I have found it is better to live a life without suspicion and mistrust.

Mark was this guy I slightly knew through the Memphis independent film community. He was a few years older than me, and although he had lived in Memphis for almost fifty years, I could tell he still considered himself an outsider. I heard he had been one of the faceless hoards of sailors-in-training based in landlocked Millington, Tennessee, a few miles north of Memphis, and had decided to stick around when his time in the military was up. To watch the groups of wide-eyed sailors walk the Memphis streets was a game for the locals, at least the locals I hung out with. At any moment, the group of eight or ten teenagers would unconsciously lock step and begin marching. Marching down a city street lined with bars and headshops, girls in tank tops and bell-bottoms. Sunglasses, new civvies, a floppy leather hippie hat, a string of beads, every manner of camouflage that could be had at the Millington PX, nothing could hide the fact that these kids were three months out of Iowa, North Dakota, West Virginia: anywhere teenage boys dream of the ocean and a life far away from wherever home happens to be.

My friend told me Mark had an art studio in a downtown warehouse, but I had never seen his work till they screened his new film at a local festival. It was a wild tale of a group of artist-bohemian-outsiders living in a warehouse district near downtown Memphis. It had a certain weird charm that puzzled me. I knew he was trying to be cutting-edge and outrageous, there was tons of cussing and belittling and harassing among the characters, but the story kept landing back into a kind of sweet tale of these misfits ultimately looking out for one another. But I knew this wasn't what he was after. That was about all I knew about him.

The fake hippie, the purloined girl, the VW van, and Carl in
West Memphis, AR, 1972

There exists a picture of a woman and two men standing by gas
pumps at a West Memphis, Arkansas filling station. The year is
1972. It is July, and the trio stands beside an older Volkswagen van.
The van, its driver a skinny Vietnam vet who didn't talk much, and
his Asian wife, who smiled at everyone but didn't say much either,
has trudged across the west from California, and picked up along
the way an unlikely assemblage of hitchhikers: a toothless man who
looked far beyond his early forties, his two little boys, one about ten
and the other not over six, plucked off the side of the hot road near
Needles, California after their car ran out of gas; and a furtive young
man who stuck close to an odd Memphis girl he stole away from
her Assembly of God Church group while on a trip to Disneyland
(he bought her a floppy leather hat, and he wore a leather headband
that shouted "fake hippie." He was most certainly a criminal and
met her in Memphis, and two days later hitchhiked all the way to
Anaheim to profess his love and perform this rude abduction); Carl
and me, worn out from a blur of rides in pickup truck beds with
silent Indians in northern New Mexico, of sleeping in a Denver
park and walking the length of Colfax Avenue, hot and hungry, only
to be thrown off the highway by a cop who threatens jail if he saw

us again, finally a ride across bleak eastern Colorado and bleaker Kansas in a Ryder rental truck with a crazy guy who let me drive when he got tired, and put us up for the night at his place in Oklahoma City and then bought us two six-packs of Coors tall-boys which we stashed in our backpacks, then seven or eight rides through scrubby east Oklahoma, eeking out a few miles at a time till the mirage of a rattle-trap VW van appeared as the sun dropped low at our backs and we could almost see Arkansas. A more bedraggled flock of pilgrims was rarely seen on the highway, and the fact we had found one another was even more of a miracle. When we laid our bedrolls out in the grass of the rest area the driver told us to look up at the stars. He said he was thankful to be alive and to be there with each one of us. I remember him saying, "Some things are meant to be." His honesty was somehow disturbing to me, bringing back all sorts of memories and regrets that led me to that moment, lying under the stars off an incessant super highway amongst strangers. The little boys were already asleep.

The sun woke us early the next morning, and each of us wandered into the woods to find a private place. The dew had laid like a blanket over our rest and was steaming in slow motion in the early morning July sunlight. Trucks were moaning out on the highway. We pulled our soggy selves into the van and took our cramped places on the floor. It took another seven hours to get across Arkansas, the long hills held our progress to forty mph, and the downhill rides made the little bus shudder and whine. We stopped for gas and food a couple of times and were treated like lepers by the people around us. It was as if they could sense the desperation and the hopelessness among us. We were the lost people. Lost in the world, holding onto vague dreams we'd bet our lives on, and heading for who knew where.

Finally, as if in a dream, we were in West Memphis, a loud place of truck drivers and motion, and I took my plastic camera out of the backpack and took a picture of Carl and the fake hippie guy and his purloined girlfriend. They look back at me as I write this, this window from fifty years ago that is as alive in my mind as it was on that July day in 1972. Who among those unlikely people crammed in a Volkswagen microbus is alive today? Maybe the two little boys? I wish I had taken a picture of all my fellow travelers that day. We crawled across the Mississippi River bridge and they let us off on Lamar Avenue and vanished into the city. I never knew where they were ultimately heading.

About forty years later I was asked to help out on a short film. My friend David asked me to shoot and edit a scene he and his buddy Mark were doing. It was one of a string of independent films I helped out with during the halcyon days of indie films when it seemed that everyone wanted to become a filmmaker and every town hosted a film festival.

When I got to Mark's house, they were going over lines, rewriting some things and figuring out where to shoot. I said my hellos and wandered around and finally decided to set up my tripod and camera in the sunroom, a nicely done room with plants and some tasteful art on the walls. As I was admiring the paintings, I noticed a photograph on a bookshelf. It was a small, faded snapshot of a young man and a young Asian woman standing by an old, even then, VW microbus. They were flanked by a sad-looking older man who was squatting, holding a little boy on his knee while another, older kid draped his arm over the man's drooped shoulders, next to them was a long-haired man sporting a headband, standing with his arm around a pensive girl in a floppy leather hat, and on the other side of the frame stood Carl and me. At a service station in West Memphis. I was stunned that I hadn't remembered someone taking our picture. Tears filled my eyes. I guess the guy, Mark, who I had sort of known for a few years was the guy who gave us that ride, the guy who said he was happy to be with each of us, lying in the wet grass along Interstate 40, looking up at the universe of stars. I started to walk into the other room and announce this bizarre turn of events, but I didn't. And I haven't. And, although I don't know why, I won't.

———○———

That day in July of 1972, when Carl and I walked up to the duplex on Dawnwood Cove, sunburned, dusty, and bone weary from our ten days on the road, we sat down in the living room and didn't say anything for a while. Finally, Carl quietly said, "I don't think I'm going to hitchhike anymore." I didn't say anything because I knew that I would.

Carl, just off the road, 1972

The Popeye Hole

My father paid Dot, (my mother's best friend and my stepfather's first cousin), fifteen dollars a week for my room and board. She always said she'd gladly do it for nothing, but she felt strongly that he needed to take some responsibility for me. He didn't come around much, maybe once a month, usually to pick me up and take me down to Port Gibson to see his brothers and sisters. They always made a point to ask after my mother, and I cheerily told them that she was happier than she'd ever been. They somehow thought that she had done him wrong when she divorced him, and abandoned me in the process. But that wasn't it at all. I had gone to North Carolina with her after she and Joe had married, but something didn't click for me. She was navigating a new life, with new children, and I wasn't happy in the least. Not because of anything she or Joe or the kids had done, but because it wasn't mine. Also, lurking in the back of my mind was the offer from Dot to come back and live with her if I didn't like it there. It took six weeks away from Rolling Fork in a new school, where I skipped school for the final three weeks anyway, before I went to my mother and asked if I could go back home. "But this is your home now. You've just got to give it a chance. You'll see." And she began to cry, knowing that it wouldn't work out, and knowing that I would be leaving. Later she told me it was the hardest thing she had ever done, to let me leave like that at seventeen years old. She felt she had let me down. But I knew there wasn't a place for me there. This was her new life, a life that proved to be the best thing she ever did for herself. Over the years, I spent some of the happiest times I can remember with them in North Carolina. They were there when I needed to come home a couple of times during my young adulthood. But in 1968, I was scared. I needed to be in Rolling Fork, near the people I knew and loved.

Her marriage to Joe was happy and lasted for over thirty-five years. My relationship with him during those many years was everything I imagined it should be. He was one of the kindest, most gentle, upright people I've ever known. He treated me like his own, sharing his goodness with me at every turn. We fished, fixed the brakes on my car, worked in the garden, and did all the things I never knew a family was supposed to do. He was a wonderful grandfather to my kids. He set an example for me that I hope I've passed on to my own children.

I rode the Greyhound bus back from the North Carolina coast all the way to Rolling Fork. It took two days and nights before the driver opened the door and I stepped out onto the Delta ground at Cecil's service station, the very place I had waited for my father when he came home from Whitfield six years earlier. It was late February and getting dark when I walked to Dot's house. She wasn't sure when I would arrive. We had made a long distance call several days before, and she and my mother had worked out the details. It's funny now to think about long distance calls and how people would only stay on the phone for a minute or two so as not to run up the bill too much. The world was a small, simple place then.

Daddy came over from Belzoni the next night and talked with Dot in private for fifteen minutes or so, then took me for a ride in his car, warning me to mind her and to help out around the house. I believe that's the first time he and I had ever had a conversation lasting more than a minute or two. He didn't really know what to say, but I think he felt like he needed to say something. He told me he would leave my five dollar a week allowance with his friend, Mr. Denton, and I could stop by his dime store to pick it up on Mondays. I was stunned that he had actually thought some of this out. He also told me that he would be coming over to pick me up on Saturday so I could spend the night with him in Belzoni, where he was working and living in a boarding house.

I slept in a bed with my father that night, the metal springs screechily groaning loudly every time he turned over after he'd wake himself up after a run of loud snoring. We had gone to the Popeye Hole earlier that night, a nondescript block building out beside Highway 49 in Belzoni, a place where mainly men congregated during the week to gamble and drink, and brought their wives on Saturday night when the band played dance music. It was about as close to a real nightclub as you could find in the Delta. A rough place nonetheless. The name had nothing to do with the cartoon character Popeye. It was named for the mutant catfish that populated the small pond beside the club, just adjacent to a cotton field where the runoff surely contained DDT and every flavor of cotton poison and weed killer known to man. The runoff had affected the fish in the pond to the point that their eyes freakishly bulged almost out of their skulls. I don't remember if they caught and served the popeye catfish at the club, but my guess is that they did, along with chitlins, oysters, crawfish and hot tamales of unknown origin. He let me drink a couple of beers, and I sat there at the table with some of his friends and their wives, and even danced with one of the wives to that song "Barefootin."

The next morning we ate breakfast at the rooming house with the other boarders. I had always heard that expression "boarding house reach" used to describe people descending on a platter of chicken or biscuits, but I saw it in action that morning. As soon as the bacon hit the table, it was gone. Biscuits...gone. It was a strange collection of men around the table, presided over by a tough little woman who put up with no foolishness. I got to know her well during the next year or so, and would sit in the kitchen while she scurried about making a meal, an unfiltered cigarette nailed into the corner of her droopy mouth, and mumbling the whole time about some real or imagined slight that happened years ago. I even visited her a couple of times after Daddy was long gone from Belzoni. She fed me each time and told me I always had a place at her table. I figured she had seen this same sad story play out a few times over the years at the boarding house.

Dr. Wilson

Dr. Bryant R. Wilson, c.1999

Dr. Wilson was my uncle by marriage. He was married to my aunt Roberta, who was about five years older than my mother. Everybody called him Dr. Wilson, even aunt Roberta. I never thought that was odd till I got older. The first time my ex-wife came to Mississippi with me, she met him. We drove the two hours over to his house for lunch and there he was, ready for the conquest. I'm sure the ladies who looked after him had gotten him up early that morning and helped him with his selected outfit, which that day consisted of a pair of red silk pajamas, a pair of logger's boots, and a polo helmet onto which he had fashioned a transistor radio and a pair of headphones. This was long before the Sony Walkman or the iPod. A man clearly ahead of his time. There were two sisters who were taking care of him, one big one and one little one. They hadn't been here the last time I had seen him. I had a feeling he didn't keep his "helpers" around too long.

When we walked into the room he acted like he was feeble, but I was onto that trick. He shook my hand and asked who that person was with me. I told him her name was Rachel and he said, "What? You know I'm deaf now. And come closer 'cause y'all know I'm mostly blind." He was not. He just wanted to get a closer look at her. I saw him cut his eyes over to me, knowing that I knew. He quickly went to task. "Say, Willy, is this the girl you had with you when you were here about a month ago?"

"Dr. Wilson, I haven't been here in over a year."

He looked at her, his eyes fairly twinkling, "Why, yes you were," he said. Dismissing me with a wave of his liver-spotted and wrinkled hand. He turned to her and said in his best, broadest, upper-class southern accent, "Willy came by here (pronouncing it 'heeya'), he was riding on a motorcycle, and some big-bosomed gal was on the back and she was hanging on real tight." He lifted his eyebrows a-la Groucho Marx, fairly leering. "Yes sir, she was hanging on *real* tight. I think they were going to New Orleans. You know, that's the city of love. I was a visitor there in 1938, had just come into the port from working on a banana boat out of British Honduras by way of Cayenne, French Guyana. You know where that is don't you? They call it something else today, but you know where that is, don't you?" She, for probably the first time in her life, was speechless. "Uh, yes, uh, that's, what's it called these days, Willy?"

"Belize." I said quietly.

The good doctor jumped right back in.

"Belize, that's right. Say, are you a Jew?" My heart sank. I knew he was in one of those moods where he just had to stir the pot, to get things going so everyone is set against everyone else and there was sure to be a fight in the offing. He loved it when that happened. A big screaming cuss-fight, where somebody slams the door on their way out then sticks their head back in the door and says something along the lines of, "Y'all can just kiss my ass, I ain't never coming back here!" I had seen it so many times before, like the time around 1976 when he announced at the supper table, my Baptist aunts and uncles picking at their food around the big dining room table, wanting to be anywhere but here, just waiting for him to get going. "Willy, do you have some marijuana?" My mother, just flown in from North Carolina that afternoon, nearly spit her iced tea across the table. "Why, no, I don't. Uh, I don't do anything like that." Never mind the John Lennon beard and hair down to my shoulders, sandals and a pair of overalls (with a peace sign patch on the bib, no less. Could I have been that much of a cliche?).

He sat up a little straighter in his chair, eyebrows arched, a gleam in his wicked eye. "Sho nuff?" he said broadly and in a mocking, high-pitched voice. Then he leaned down on his elbows, turned his head and glared at me with a sardonic smile. "Oh, I bet you do. I'd smoke some right now if you pulled it out. Go ahead."

My uncle Chester tried to diffuse the situation, "Now, Doc, ha, ha, you know that stuff is dangerous. We don't need you getting hooked on that stuff and going all hippie on us," winking at me as he tried to laugh it off.

"Why, Chester, you don't know what you're talking about. You must mean LSD, and I'd take that too. Willy, do you have some LSD?" and on and on till my aunt Phoebe made an excuse about having to get back to the house before Bertie got finished with his night chores. This she explained while walking out the door, effectively letting everyone else around the table know that it was OK to take their leave even though the mashed potatoes were still steaming hot and people had barely touched their food. "Come on Vaughn, we've got to get," my aunt Hazel said, pulling Vaughn away from the table. "Sweetheart, I ain't hardly eat anything yet," uncle Vaughn said in a disappointed way (he hadn't been paying attention to any of the proceedings). "Vaughn," my aunt said, emphatically. He got up and sheepishly began walking toward the door. Doc began, in his patented country voice, "Well, Vaughn, I can't believe you let Hazel talk to you like that. What kind of man are you? Boy, all she has to do is snap her fingers and you're steppin' and fetchin'. Damn if I know how you put up with it. But don't worry, I promise I won't tell the boys down at the barbershop how henpecked she's got you. Lord have mercy!" He flung his napkin toward the middle of the table.

Uncle Vaughn looked around the room like he knew what was coming. "Now, Doc, that ain't no way to talk about Hazel, she's your wife's sister and all. And we do have to get on home too. AND, I don't care a whit about what you tell that bunch of easy-riders and alcoholics that hang around that dang barbershop. It ain't none of their business how Hazel and me talks." Doc eased back in his chair, a satisfied grin came over his face and he said, "Honey, pass me them peas, all of a sudden I'm hungry as a big ole bear." A near perfect symphony for the good doctor. His execution and conducting flawless, and even though it was almost like child's play to him, he relished every moment of it, and truth be known, had probably been planning this performance for days.

I had tried to prepare Rachel for the doctor, but I quickly realized I had forgotten the skill and deft by which he played the game. Get them off balance, mixed up, thinking that he's crazy, but in a funny, harmless sort of way, then go for the jugular by setting everyone against one another as he sits back and basks in the bizarre outcome. "So, are you a Jew?" he glanced at me to gauge if I was mad or merely resigned to the inevitable. "Why, yes, I am Jewish. My family came over in 1938, just before the war in Europe started. We were German Jews. Berlin. My father was twenty and had just begun to work in a bank with his father. They got out just before things got crazy. Much of our family was not so lucky. I had over a hundred family members, cousins and aunts and uncles, murdered in the concentration camps."

"They wouldn't let me go over to fight. I had to stay right here 'cause I was the only doctor in this county, but I wanted to go. Say y'all owned a bank? The Jews around here all own the banks, but I don't 'spect they have as much money as me." He grinned at me. "I only keep a maximum of fifty thousand in each bank account. I got hurt pretty bad when the banks closed down in '32. Ole Roosevelt was slick, but he did start that FDIC to protect your money, that is, up to fifty thousand dollars. I've got accounts in banks all over Mississippi." He leaned in to whisper. "Don't tell these old gals, or they'll try to find out where all my money is. I believe they're stealing from me." The woman nearest me rolled her eyes, having heard everything. "They did take me to Hawaii," except he pronounced it *Hi-wah-yuh*, "and I taught everybody over there how to do the modified hula. Boy, they didn't know what to think about me! Yeah, they dressed me up in a grass skirt and made me do the modified hula." He was hinting for someone to ask how it's done, so I offered, "Just exactly how is the modified hula performed?" Rachel shot me a pained look.

"Well, you don't know nothin'. I thought you knew about everything. I thought you were the big writer. Here, I'll show you." To the smallest lady, "Here, what's your name again? Go put on that record that I like to hula to."

"Bernice." The big woman said.

"What?"

"Doc, you know her name is Bernice. She's my sister."

"Well, who are you?"

"I'm Janelle. You know good and well who I am. You delivered me and Bernice."

"I don't believe I've ever seen you before today. Who sent y'all over here?" he said.

"Lord have mercy!" She threw her hands up and walked to the record player.

That record he liked to hula to was Fats Domino's "I'm Walking."

"Where's my hula skirt?" He stood up.

They went into the bedroom and brought out the grass hula skirt, and by the time they got it on him they had to start the record over. And with that he began this insane-looking shuffle and bending of his knees while he was kind of unfurling his arms in front of his chest. He had to have been making it up on the spot. Rachel began to laugh out loud.

This reaction really got him going, and he began to add little flourishes with his hands, all the while cutting his eyes to everyone in the room to judge how he was doing. When the song was over he sat down heavily in his chair, huffing and puffing, but clearly delighted in his performance.

"I did that in front of three hundred people in Hawaii. They wanted me to do it every night, but I wasn't up to it. I think they want me to come back. They recognized that I was a professional dancer." Except he said, in his best British accent, "Dahncer," which suddenly reminded me of the time I was visiting him and Aunt Roberta when I was about nine, and she had sat me on the "breeze-way," this long room with windows all around, with a bowl of fresh cherries.

I can't remember what I was thinking, but I put a cherry pit up my nose and couldn't get it out. I went outside behind the garage and tried with all my might to blow the thing out of my nose. I even tried to pry it loose with a stick, but it just kept going further and further up my nose. Finally, after about an hour of frantically trying to get rid of this thing, I had to go in the house and tell her what I had done. "You did what? We've got to go to the clinic." And we drove in the car to the town square where Dr. Wilson had his clinic. We parked and went in. The waiting room was filled with country folks suffering from cuts, broken arms, old age, mumps and measles. She whisked me back to see the good doctor. "You did what?"

"I put a cherry pit up my nose."

"Well, why did you do that?"

"Here," and with that he put a small metal thing in my nostril, and out popped my cherry pit. The whole thing hadn't lasted more than sixty seconds.

He was laughing and telling everyone what I had done when we walked back through the waiting room. When we got to the door of the clinic, he noticed a man parked outside in an old flatbed truck. The man was selling watermelons. Doctor Wilson walked up to the man and said, "Ceph, how many melons you got on that truck?"

The man looked at the load. "I figure I got about seventy five, Doc."

"What'll you take for the whole bunch?"

"What you gon do with all them melons, Doc?"

"I want to buy the whole load."

"Every one of 'em?"

"Yessir, how much you need?"

"I'd figure about four bits a piece."

"Sold. How about I give you forty for the whole bunch?' He pulled an enormous wad of cash from his pants pocket and whipped off two twenties. "Now, I need you to stand here and hand them out to people who come by."

"Give 'em away?"

"Yeah, just everybody that comes along, ask if they want a melon. Give 'em two if they want 'em." The man nodded his head and went about his business.

"Ceph, give the first one to this boy here." He motioned to me.

The man handed me a nice round melon, and aunt Roberta and I began walking toward her car.

"Hey!" the doctor yelled when we were a sufficient way down the sidewalk. "Don't put that up your nose!"

I realized at that moment, at nine years old, that he was different. That his money and position made him different, or had given him some sort of permission to do as he liked, and that maybe he was a little crazy. I remember thinking, *"They all shake their heads and don't know what to make of him, but they respect him, and even if they don't respect him, they fear him a little, like they don't quite know what he's going to do next. And that's power. He bought all those melons just to holler down the street at me to not put one up my nose."*

That memory came to me, but it wasn't the memory I had from his saying, *"Dahnce."* That was when I was about twelve and he and I were going into the drug store for a milkshake, and just before we got to the door he stopped me, bent down to my eye level and said, "When we go in there, you speak with an English accent."

"But Dr. Wilson, I don't know how to do that."

"Yes you can, just do it."

So we walked into the crowded drugstore and *HE* started speaking in an English accent. The people in the drug store didn't pay much attention to this. They got the good doctor every day.

Still huffing and puffing from the modified hula, but clearly in a state of euphoria, all eyes were on him and he loved it. After a minute or two he started to twiddle his thumbs and I could see that he was wanting to stir the pot again. He looked at the little woman. "Say, where's that daughter of yours?" And then to me. "You know, she's trying to marry off her daughter to me. Now, she looks alright, but I believe she's been out behind the barn a few times, if you know what I mean." And with that, he gave a broad theatrical wink to Rachel.

The little woman reacted with horror. "Now, Doc, Helen ain't been over here but one time and you embarrassed her so that she won't come back." To me, "I had to meet her up at the dollar store parking lot last time she come. She won't even come out here no more."

He shrugged his shoulders grandly, "Say what you will, but that gal was giving me the eye."

"She wadn't giving nobody the eye." She turned to me, "She was born with what they call a lazy eye and has kind of a twitch, and Doc here kept thinking she was winkin' at him."

"She said she wanted to go to Hawaii with me!"

"No she didn't, she said she'd like to go someday."

"Well, I think she was giving me the eye, and y'all are trying to figure out some way I'll marry her so y'all can get my money."

The big sister jumped in, "Doc, we ain't studying your money, and you're talking about my favorite niece, she's already married and got kids too."

"Yeah, but y'all said her husband drove a pulpwood truck and drank up his paycheck every week."

By this point in the conversation Rachel had leaned in so far I thought she might fall out of her chair. Turning to Rachel, he said, "Willy's mama used to get mad at me 'cause I said that he was just like me. I went over there to the Delta to see him one time, and all he wanted to do was stand around and chew the fat with poor white trash and nigras. Now what do you think about that?" Rachel stiffened.

He leaned back in his wheelchair, "So, Willy, how many times have you been married?"

"Dr. Wilson, you know I've never been married."

"Well, your aunt Mabel was saying just the other day that you must be gay. I told her I didn't think so, but I'd ask you the next time I saw you. I guess Rachel could fill us in on that story, couldn't she?" He wiggled his eyebrows at her. She sat up in her chair. All eyes were on her.

"I caught him wearing one of my dresses a few weeks ago, and trying on my high heels, but I don't think he's gay...or very gay." This brought the house down. The sisters flew into a fit of relieved laughter. Rachel had sparred with the master and had held her own. I had survived another withering visit with him. Only he, sitting there chuckling, was unsatisfied. He had wanted something bigger, something more explosive, something to remember. But there would be other days and other people to conquer.

About a year and a half after our visit, Bernice, the little one, called to say that Dr. Wilson had passed during the night. She said, "I don't know what happened to him. He had been feeling poorly the last few days, but last night he was back to his old self. He was talking about you and that girl you brought with you that last time you were here. I think he took a shine to her. He made Janelle put on some records, and he even tried to get up and dance. Me and Janelle are gonna miss Doc. He sure was a pill."

The next day, I flew into Jackson and drove to his house. The only people there were Bernice and Janelle, no relatives or friends. I was pretty sure Doc had run off most of his old friends and surely all of the relatives who might still be living. I was also sure there would be people coming out of the woodwork to try and get their hands on some of his money, but being the executor of his estate, I knew he had run through most of it and figured I would just give the little was left to Janelle and Bernice. After all, they had stuck with him through more than two years of his constant belittling, cajoling, and troublemaking. That had to be worth something.

Mr. Faulkner

William Faulkner's writing room, Rowan Oak, Oxford, Mississippi.

In Mr. Faulkner's novel, *Light in August,* we are introduced, on the opening page, to a character named Lena Grove, who is walking, nine months pregnant, from Alabama to Mississippi, in search of the father of her soon-to-be-born chap. She says in the opening scene as well as the very end of the book, "My, my, a body does get around," as if astonished by where she's been in her relatively short, cloistered life. She walks on in faith that her goal is just around the next bend, or in the next town, but always forward in an inexorable pilgrimage toward her destiny. I have felt that exact feeling throughout my life, so much so that I am very seldom surprised or unprepared. I have come to expect the serendipity that is my life, and to embrace it as my gift from the Universe.

"A failed poet" was the way Mr. Faulkner described himself. I always wondered if this was just another outward manifestation of his narcissism or if he really believed it. That he felt he had let himself down by not being able to capture in a few well constructed lines what it later took millions of words and sentences seems slightly disingenuous to me. He carefully curated his character to set himself apart from his fellows. He didn't like to talk about writing, or his books, or his methods. He, instead, chose to seek the company of his hunting buddies who had never, and would never, read his books, and thus, never question him as to his motives or approach. During his time as writer-in-residence at the University of Virginia, he was forced to talk about his writing, but I'm convinced he weighed that against the fact that his daughter and grandsons, whom he loved dearly, lived in Charlottesville, and somebody was housing and paying him to assent to questioning. It was the easiest path forward. I imagine him smugly thinking to himself, "My, my, a body does get around."

Faulkner's home is my personal Mecca. I go there whenever I'm in Oxford, and have been there dozens and dozens of times. I consider him the greatest writer in the English language. His work makes sense to me on every level.

I've found that people like to be informed, even considered expert, but don't care much for the work involved. One morning I was standing on the porch at Mr. Faulkner's house, Rowan Oak, waiting for the door to open at 10 am. There was an older couple waiting there as well. The wife looked at the husband and said, in a clearly Iowan or Nebraskan accent, "Murray, Faulkner wrote 'For Whom the Bell Tolls,' didn't he?" I shot a glance at Murray. He looked back at me. I narrowed my eyes and shook my head, almost imperceptibly, and I think I may have mouthed the word "Hemingway." At least in my mind I did.

Murray looked down at his feet and said, "Yeah, I think so."

I don't know why that chaps my ass, but it does. To be fair, I guess when you find yourself in Oxford, you go to Faulkner's. When you find yourself in Memphis, you go to Elvis' house; West Branch, Iowa, you've got to go to Herbert Hoover's. I don't need to be such a snob about this.

Charles Crawford, a most agreeable gentleman and famous professor of history in Memphis, once took me aside and told me he had known Mr. Faulkner in the '50s and early '60s. His best story detailed a dinner to which he had been invited at the home of another Ole Miss professor on a Wednesday night years before. Faulkner showed up unannounced at the front door and proceeded to sit down to watch *Car 54, Where Are You?* After the program ended, with very little said, Faulkner left to walk home, and the professor told his guest, "Mr. Bill won't have a television set at Rowan Oak, but he comes over here every Wednesday night to watch his program. He thinks it's the best thing on."

Faulkner didn't like anyone coming to see him unannounced or announced for that matter. He guarded his privacy with the stubbornness and intransigence of one who had lost or had personal privacy suspended in some way. No matter that people had traveled long distances, or that they were of eminent stature in the literary *milieu*, the Nobel laureate simply would decline to see them. Once, just after John F. Kennedy was elected president, Faulkner was invited to the White House for a dinner honoring a number of Nobel Prize recipients. He declined, saying something to the effect of, "That's a mighty long way to go just to eat supper."

During my brief sojourn at Ole Miss in 1971, I stopped going to class in late October, and began riding my bike out to Rowan Oak. It was a medium-sized country house that pretended to be a mansion, unadorned but for the columns at the front, and rough-hewn inside with single wall construction and a clapboard exterior.

From a distance it looked like a great mansion. An Ole Miss work-study student dutifully watched over the house for some elusive reason, since there were rarely any visitors. I spent many long autumn afternoons at Rowan Oak.

The student was a pleasant sort, one of those guys who had gotten into a fraternity but couldn't quite run with the big dogs when it came to spending money and wearing the latest fashions, hence, he worked, or more correctly, he sat in the downstairs hallway reading his psychology textbook or the Kappa Sig handbook. He generally paid no attention to me as I nosed around the house. Our conversations remained brief.

"Hey, man, can I look through some of Mr. Bill's books?"

"Yeah, but if anyone comes in, don't let them see you opening the books."

or

"Hey, man, can I touch Mr. Bill's typewriter?"

"Yeah, you can sit in his chair if you want to, just don't break anything."

So, on through the fall afternoons I wandered Faulkner's house, studying the phone numbers he had written in pencil on the kitchen wall by the telephone, the mud still on his hunting boots in his upstairs closet, his alarm clock on the bedside table, his writing room with the two single beds and the outline for "A Fable" written on the wall in a child's crayon, little signs of life in a house absent its master for nearly ten years. Sitting in his chair, a rustic straight-backed chair with a woven wicker seat, my fingers on the keys of the typewriter, I could feel the joy and frustration of his life, the loveless marriage, the constant intrusions from a growing throng of admirers and scholars for whom he neither had patience nor the slightest interest in sharing conversation. He was a man beset with the ghosts of his past, the fabrication of his time in the Royal Canadian Air Force during the first world war, the ridicule he endured at the hands of his townsmen, the drinking, ah, the drinking, that nearly killed him on so many occasions, the cycle of binges and drying out in the Byhalia sanatorium, all from the greatest writer in the English language.

What demons must have inhabited his days and nights. His literary output was unparalleled, but what could he have done if people had only left him alone as he so desired. He liked to think of himself as a gentleman farmer, and I guess he achieved a lot of that in his later years: fox hunting in Virginia astride a horse, strolling the storied campus as writer-in-residence, and making diplomatic trips for the Department of State. He was written out by the time he wrote "The Town," "The Mansion," and "The Reivers," his best work having come in the 1930s, where he toiled night and day, trying to figure out how to pay the bills, while continuing to do what he was driven, destined to do. He knew he was completely unsuited for any normal kind of work. His job as postmaster at the university had been a disaster, earning him the enmity of students and faculty alike, and only adding to his reputation of being an oddball and a dilettante. There was no turning back. Hollywood was a godsend, and he managed to hang around and contribute dialogue to a string of great movies. But he never liked being a screenwriter. It was too confining, too rigid, too collaborative. He longed to get back to Oxford, his little postage stamp of land in North Mississippi to continue the saga of Yoknapatawpha. And to hide.

He hunted in the south Delta and looked forward to coming to the Big Woods every autumn for long days and nights of stalking deer and eating venison around the campfire. Stories suggest that once the seal had been broken on a bottle of bourbon, the top was flung into the fire, assuring the bottle be emptied.

On one of those trips to the Delta, he was in a cafe eating breakfast when word got to my friend's father, Hal DeCell, who was a young newspaperman, that the great man was in town. Since Faulkner had recently been informed of winning the Nobel Prize for literature, the young newspaperman ran to the cafe and spent a few frustrating minutes trying to interview the reluctant writer. Sensing that he was bothering Faulkner, Mr. DeCell announced that he had one last question. "What's your favorite book you've written, Mr. Bill?" Without batting an eye Faulkner replied, "Lanterns on the Levee," and off ran the young man to put his scoop into the weekly paper that was being printed that day. As the last copy of the paper came off the printing press, Hal DeCell realized that "Lanterns on the Levee" had been written some years before by Greenville poet and author William Alexander Percy.

Archie Manning Is Not Clumsy

Willy Bearden, Rolling Fork Colonels, 1967

If there was one thing the Delta revolved around, other than cotton and whiskey, it was high school football. From an early age, all able-bodied males were prepared for a six-year career on the gridiron. We paid so much attention to and spent so much time on the game that I assumed there would be a job awaiting me in the football business at some point in the future. That never worked out. In fact, I don't think but a couple of guys ever made it past playing over at Moorhead, aka Mississippi Delta Junior College, aka Harvard on the Highway.

It was as if the adults of Rolling Fork might have said, "We might be sitting in the ass-end of one of the poorest and most ridiculed sections of the country. We might be the smallest school in the conference. We might be diligently trying to perpetuate the 'separate but equal' nonsense of the bizarre, alter universe of anti-civil rights, but we will absolutely and without question *kick your ass on the football field.*"

Football was the bane of my existence. My memories go back to cold afternoons in the early spring, wet and exhausted, on the bottom of a pile of idiots who would step on your shins or your back, and the pain would radiate through your body just as the coach said something like, "Weak. Pitiful. Let's do it again." Or having to show up for weightlifting and running in the summer after working all day in the cotton fields. It was a huge commitment of time and energy, but there was no way to not play and still live in Rolling Fork.

My one moment of glory on the football field came in the fall of 1966, when I was a 16 year-old sophomore. We had ridden the school bus the 75 miles to Drew, Mississippi for a Friday night game. We piled off the bus carrying our helmets and shoulder pads and began walking to the cramped visitors' locker room under the stands. In the parking lot, just by the gate, was a 1948 or '49 Dodge, painted bright orange (the school colors) with "007" painted on the driver's side door in blue. Just inside the gate, sitting on a wooden table, eating from a bag of chocolate chip cookies, was the best athlete in the Delta: Archie Manning. He regarded us with a smile and a nod as we passed silently by his perch. We had all seen him in action, running the high hurdles at a track meet, leaving everyone else in the dust, pitching a baseball by you so fast it made your eyes hurt, hitting 40 foot jump shots on the basketball court with an ease that made you want to give up and go home. But on the football field he was something else. He could throw a spiral sixty yards with such beauty and ease that, try as you might, you simply couldn't hate him. His only problem was that you knew he was going to carry the ball, or when he threw it, most of the time it would bounce off his tiny receivers. It must have been frustrating for him to play on teams that never won the big games. As much as we respected him, really were in awe of him, we were still going to beat the snot out of him that night. That was a foregone conclusion.

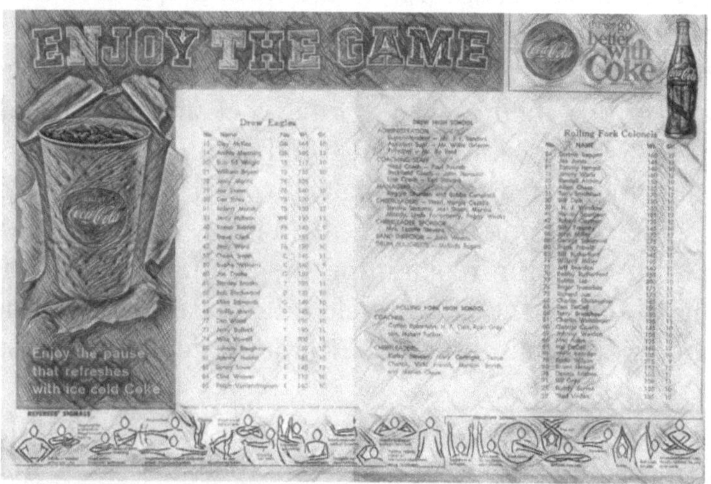

Game program, Rolling Fork Colonels vs. Drew Eagles, 1966

The game went as we expected, and we were up 28 to 10, or somewhere thereabouts, deep in the third quarter. Actually, we were pretty stunned that they had scored that much against us. We were used to "skunking" teams. Archie had played his heart out that night, running the quarterback option so many times that the only question was which side it was coming to next. Coach Robertson put me in at the end of the third quarter. "Don't you let him get outside you!" he said fiercely as I ran onto the field. I was a defensive end, all 146 pounds of me. On my second play in the game, Archie rolled right and there I was, waiting for him to pitch the ball to his halfback or tuck it and turn up the field. I will never say I tackled Archie Manning, but in that moment, he pulled the football in, lowered his head, and somewhere in the melee he got tangled up in my feet as he ran over me, and he went down. Everybody was slapping me on the back because I had "tackled" Archie Manning. The truth is, I may have even been running away from Archie. That is all I have to say about football.

Well, maybe not all. As I was thinking about those days and all the time and energy we put into practicing football, I thought that for all they talked about the communist threat during the sixties, they sure had us thinking like Bolsheviks. The idea of individuality was a sin on the football field. It was all about team. All about the collective. We went to football camp for a week each summer at an FFA camp over in Grenada, and butted heads twice a day in the withering sun and 90% humidity. Of course, this was during the time when they thought that drinking water was dangerous for you, or at least a sign of weakness if you asked for water, and they handed out salt tablets like M&Ms. But we were the Colonels, the lords of the football field, the toughest bunch of country boys in Mississippi.

On Thursday nights at football camp, we would have what they called "dedication night," a chance for each person on the team to stand in front of the group and state, out loud what they intended to do, or what the team meant to them, or to bury the hatchet with some teammate. From the time I was in the ninth grade, I sat through four of these "come to Jesus" sessions, and heard boys cry like babies while talking about how much they loved the team. Some boys would break down completely and begin talking about things that happened in their homes, and the brutality and hopelessness they faced in their lives. It was a strange, unpredictable opera being played out in the dining hall of a Future Farmers of America camp in the hills of Mississippi. Looking back now, it seems like the most bizarre mind game I can imagine, and shame on those grown men for manipulating us with such abandon. I remember in 1978, when Jim Jones and his folks in Guyana committed mass suicide, and people were shocked and couldn't understand how something like that had happened. I'm not saying the football team was anything like the People's Church, but I knew exactly how it had happened and how it could happen easily, and with virtually anyone. The power of the group, especially in isolation and stress, is as astounding as it is frightening. I wish I could trade the hours I spent on the football field for hours learning the piano or maybe reading. This is not to say that sports have no place; I love football and watch the NFL with gusto. I love the fact that Archie Manning's sons, Peyton and Eli, are great players who have taken the game to new heights. But for the best times in your life to have happened all in the three or four years you played high school football is pretty disturbing. The joke around Rolling Fork is, "Know how to spot a Colonel?"

"No, how?"

"Watch for the guys who are limping."

It's true. So many of my teammates have blown-out knees and arthritis in their hands and feet. For many of them, it was worth the price they paid. After forty and fifty years, conversations still drift to the football field, and so many of my teammates still remember the scores of the games and who did what. I only remember Archie.

The Society of Alcoholism

I grew up in a society of alcoholism. It didn't help matters that the sale of alcohol was strictly prohibited in every county in Mississippi. That fact only made it more desirable. Beer joints and roadhouses flourished in every county, run by the worst of us, quietly sanctioned by the city/county governments, profited from by law enforcement, and perpetuated by the Baptist Church.

Our local roadhouse was Polly's Place, sitting by itself at the intersection of Highway 1 and Highway 14, about five miles west of Rolling Fork. It was a low-slung building with requisite Falstaff and Jax beer neon signs announcing the obvious, a wide Coca Cola sign with 'Polly's Place' painted in green letters and a Coke logo at each end, and a large parking lot in the rear for those who didn't want to readily advertise their whereabouts. Polly was said to be a tough woman with a heart of gold. My mama fixed her hair for many years and counted her as a friend, though Polly never came to our house for coffee. I would love to know the origin of her establishment and just how she came to host gambling and bootlegging right under the noses of the politicians, law enforcement officers, and the churches. I guess at that time in Mississippi they figured that anything that wasn't a nuisance or a direct threat to proper society was alright. And truth be told, Polly's was probably one of the safer places to frequent. Up the road in Greenville and down the road in Vicksburg were joints of greater danger and menace.

Our crop of alcoholics ran the gamut of humanity, but for most of my childhood and adolescence, the World War II veterans in our town made up the majority of the victims/practitioners. Looking back on those times, I now realize those men were in their late teens to early thirties when the war came about, and the shock of being away from home, the horror and boredom of war affected these men in ways from which they would never recover. Those were the men who drove fast, lived hard, had multiple girlfriends outside their marriages, and died in their forties and fifties. There wasn't much said about the war back then, not anywhere near how these days we talk about the Greatest Generation and the heroes who saved the world from facism. That's all a recent phenomenon, and most of the soldiers who were really haunted and destroyed by combat were long dead by the time the accolades and homages began being passed so freely around. The Greatest Generation came home with more baggage than one can imagine, and the fact they never talked openly about it is a tribute to the job Uncle Sam did on these young people. Real men aren't whiners.

One of my earliest memories is driving down Washington Street in Vicksburg, my father behind the wheel of the '56 Oldsmobile, pulling behind this nondescript building where Mr. Goula would hand out a pint of Early Times or Old Taylor or Yellowstone through one of those slots in the backdoor like in the old movies about speakeasies. My father would get me to climb over the seat and say to the slot, "Hey Mr. Goula!" and they would laugh, my father and the faceless man behind the slot. I'm sure it was some Italian slur or curse word, but that was my job every time we went to Vicksburg. Now that I think of it, we did the same thing at the East Prong Store just outside town, not say Mr. Goula, but we pulled behind there and were handed the bottle by a man known only as Dalton. On those rides, my father would let me have the last sip out of his bottle of beer. I loved the taste of that last sip of beer, followed by a crisp, salty pork rind. He would make me sit in the floorboard of the front seat so no one would see a little kid drinking from a can of Falstaff. We made all the stops, the Bear Camp Store on Highway 61 where Teddy Roosevelt is said to have camped nearby while on his famous bear hunt in 1903, the Starlight Supper Club in Delta, Louisiana, just across the river from Vicksburg, this place in Yazoo City, known to me only as the Greek's Place, and the myriad Black juke joints on backroads and in back alleys from here to Greenville and down nearly to Natchez. The Green Frog, Hattie's Cafe, Jimmy's Hot Spot, the Shakerag Inn, and on and on. I became a legend when I began my drinking career years later for being able to find a place that sold beer no matter where we were in the Delta. I was like a walking Google of beer joints way back in the sixties. I could probably still find where they were these many years later, but they're all gone now, most of Mississippi's counties having gone wet over fifty years ago. It's as easy to buy beer as it is corn flakes.

Dust, Then Mud

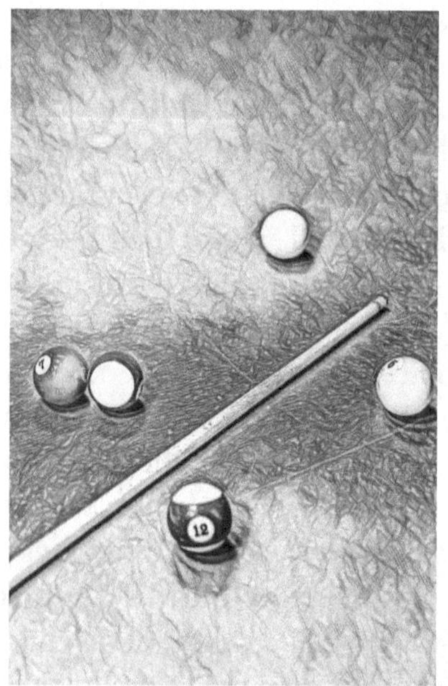

The word in the pool hall was that if a woman wanted to give you some, she would offer to shake your hand, and then tickle your palm with her middle finger. I waited my entire adolescence for that to happen. I kept thinking that the women I knew probably hadn't heard of this tradition or I surely would have had occasion to have sex with a woman. It seemed all so simple, so straightforward. Everybody wants to do it. It's just in the asking, the move, that things get sketchy.

One of my first lessons in sex came from Otha Monroe, the town drunk, or one of them anyway. I must've been about twelve. So Monroe told me, "Didn't nothin' but a puff of dust come out the first time after I hadn't had no coochie for about a year, then the next time some mud came out. I was all stopped up." My eyes grew wide and I tried to picture a puff of dust coming out of his old, decrepit pecker. That worried me for a long time. But the thing that really stayed with me for a long time, obviously till today, was the treatment for the clap. The pool hall boys held an impromptu seminar one afternoon after someone announced that Carl had gotten the clap from Sara Duncan. With everyone chiming in with their own clap story (they all seemed to have one, and most included Sara), the brutalities of the treatment took center stage. "Old Doc Barfield got me to pull ole Rudy out and lay it on the table."

"Must've been a short table." Laughs all around.

"Screw you, Jasper!"

"I'm just funnin' with you, you don't need to get all mad."

"I'm tellin' a damn story here. So, Doc looks down at that poor excuse for a pecker and says real quiet, 'You know what's comin.' And he pulls out that rubber mallet and rares back and hits ole Rudy right on the head. Pus and blood came flyin' out the end, and damn almighty it hurt."

"That ain't what he done with me and mine. He run a little rattail file up my pee hole and gouged it out for a minute. Now if you want some goddamn pain, son..."

"Burton, that ain't nothin' compared to the mallet. I've had that file thang done before."

And so, through the afternoon they drank beer, smoked cigarettes and argued the merits of treatment for venereal diseases. They were experts. Every time I hear people say we shouldn't teach sex education in our schools, I remember my panel of intellectuals and how they helped shape my knowledge of sexually transmitted diseases and their treatment. Note to self: Stay away from Sara Duncan.

Early on, I realized I had a knack for listening to people from all walks of life and then be able to replicate their speech patterns and their rhythm. I know this came from my upbringing in the Delta, hanging around the beauty shop where my mother worked when I was a kid, and later, being in the pool hall most of my waking hours. I was a listener. I really learned to read by poring over the Photoplay magazine that came to the beauty shop every week. By the time I was twelve I could recite every trashy detail that had happened in the Eddie Fisher/Debbie Reynolds/Elizabeth Taylor/Richard Burton saga. I learned to be quiet so ladies who were getting their hair rolled would forget I was sitting right there and they would go on about who was having affairs with whom, and which man had gotten thrown out of the house for coming home drunk.

If the beauty shop comprised the bulk and breadth of my undergraduate work, the pool hall was my graduate school. By the time I was fourteen I was a regular. It wasn't that hard either. The first few times I ventured inside was on the pretense of looking for someone I knew, who, clearly, wasn't there. Those first times I briefly hung around the counter, taking it all in, the big jars of pickled pig's feet and pickled eggs, the long Coke coolers filled with beer of every kind: Jax, Falstaff, Schlitz, Miller High Life, Budweiser and Busch.

They were a ragged bunch, those seemingly permanent denizens of the smoke-stained walls and dim front windows which let in so little light as to not be windows at all. Renfro, Jim T., Carl, and the king of them all, the proprietor of that dark, hallowed pit, perched just across the street from the courthouse, Marvin. If Mr. Faulkner hadn't identified the Snopes family many years before, I would swear he spent his days in the pool hall in Rolling Fork. Before you knew it, I had taken to helping Marvin out in the pool hall. I racked balls and collected the fifteen cents per game, sold pickled eggs, pig's feet and Polish sausages from the giant glass jars on the bar, and even sold beer when he was absent on one of his regular drinking binges. He never actually went anywhere, but he'd drink until he could barely stand, then go back and lay down on the back pool table and sleep for seven or eight hours, wake up and do it all over again. He was regular with the binges, about once every three months you could count on him being absent for a week to ten days. Then he'd wake up one day, take a good bath, brush his teeth, walk over to Robert A.'s, get a haircut and a shave, come back smelling of hair tonic and soap, like nothing had ever happened. His boys would help out some, but generally they stole him blind of the nickels they collected from the pool players. They didn't dare take the beer money because they knew when he sobered up he'd do a count of the beer, and being a known roughneck to begin with, they really didn't want to push it.

The pool hall regulars were a beautiful pack of alcoholics, know-it-alls, bored farmers and henpecked husbands with nowhere else to go. They congregated in the dark, smoky environs, weighing in on all subjects, taking on all comers. I learned most of what I know about women, politics, relationships, gambling, literature (they were, to a man, fans of the western, with Argosy and Swank magazines thrown in for good measure, current events, and a monthly rehashing of World War II), hunting, farming, race relations, religion, sex, and partying, right there in the pool hall. And I listened with the same determination and awe as I had around the corner in the beauty shop. That is, until one day when I was about seventeen, and I realized, like a bolt of lightning had struck me, that they were mostly unemployed alcoholics, and I probably didn't need to be taking it all as the gospel. I remember that moment as if it happened last week. I went outside and sat on the curb, watching the cars slowly orbit the town square; there was Brother Keyser in his '64 Olds, going to the hospital to visit the sick, Mrs. Truesdale heading to the grocery store, Mrs. Carter going to pick up Buzz after band practice, Burl Yelverton coming home from the elastics factory, and I knew that I had to get out of there. I don't know if I ever had the thought of living elsewhere. Maybe I assumed I would always live right there around the people I had known all my life, work at a job that someone had vacated for me, go to church every Sunday morning and Wednesday night, join the Lions Club and become the "tail twister" like my own father. But I knew in that instant that I would have to leave. It was as if someone had pulled back a curtain and I could see out a window, or as they called them back then, a picture window. After that moment life would not be the same for me.

The Old Man and the Jailhouse

How I remember Mr. McNeil.

The first time I saw a person get shot was on the front yard of the Sharkey County Courthouse, across from the pool hall. It was nothing like the thousands of cowboys or gangsters I'd seen get it at the Joy Theater down the street. This time, old man McNeil grabbed his pistol when the prisoner tried to break away, and failing to get it out of the holster, lifted his leg up and aimed at the man's knee and shot. That was all there was to it.

One shot, then the man writhed on the ground screaming like a spoiled child while Mr. McNeil hurriedly got the leather band unsnapped from the holster and stood, dancing around the squirming victim like a kid who'd taken his first buck. We stood there, across the street, in amazement. No one uttered a word, or even looked away to the other boys who were standing there. I kept thinking he was going to shoot him again. That old man had probably waited for this moment his whole career, or maybe not. Maybe he had shot other people. We would never know, because the old man was a taciturn fellow who brooked no foolishness, and none of us boys were brave enough to ever bring up the subject with him.

He rarely came into the pool hall, but when he did, Marvin, the proprietor, nodded to him as if there was some kind of agreement between them, turned and handed him a cold bottle of Jax beer and went on about his business. I would see Mr. McNeil, the town jailer, sitting in the doorway of the jailhouse in the late evenings, leaning back in a cane-bottomed chair, rolling Prince Albert loose tobacco into an OCB rolling paper, taking care to twist the ends just so, then holding it in his mouth for a long time till he finally reached under the chair, striking a kitchen match on the front leg, holding it till the flame settled, and taking a long pull on his freshly-built cigarette. Time meant nothing to him. After seeing so many people languish in the jailhouse, he knew that time was a relative thing, and not to be questioned.

He and his family, a wife and several grandkids, lived in the old railroad hotel just across the tracks from the now closed depot. The hotel fascinated me for some reason. It had been built while the Illinois Central railway laid the tracks from Memphis to Vicksburg in the 1880s, making the long trip on the small paddlewheel steamers that plied the rivers and creeks a thing of the past. Suddenly, riders and merchandise could be delivered to plantation sidings and small towns all up and down the Delta. Riding by on my bicycle, I would wonder who the guests had been in this now rickety old barn of a hotel. I never had the nerve to ask to go inside, and that is one of the great regrets of my life. As I've aged, I have learned so much and had my existence broadened by doing exactly that, asking questions, asking permission, and asking to hear people's stories. The fact is that most people want to talk about themselves, but no one ever asks. We live in a society that is increasingly driven by the idea that people don't want to know details about your life and your experience, and that it is the height of disrespect to pry into their private lives. Even with all the good things it has brought about, the make-believe world we create for ourselves on social media has done many of us a huge disservice.

The last time I saw Mr. McNeil he was standing in the doorway of the jail. It had just been announced that the city was building a new jail and that things would be modernized and even include air conditioning for the inmates. I knew his days were numbered. Although I never had a conversation with the old man, there was something unspoken between us. He looked at me as I drove by, and gave me an almost imperceptible nod. Later, I heard the whole bunch, kids and grandkids, had moved maybe to Vicksburg. I never saw him again.

Have Mercy

Walking The Dog, Rufus Thomas, 1963

Mercy Clauson married a Black woman after he moved north to Detroit in the late sixties. To say that he was making some kind of statement was far from the truth. Mercy marched to his own drummer, and seemed to know exactly what he wanted out of life. He had been a rogue and a cut-up all his life, and this marriage, while still a shock in Rolling Fork, was certainly in line with his previous behavior. The boys in the pool hall always respected him, even as a teenager. Everything would stop momentarily when he entered. "Have Mercy!" they'd shout, and he would get this self-satisfied smile and walk to the jukebox and play something like the Hombres' "Let It All Hang Out," while the men looked on with some kind of twisted yet bemused admiration. Mercy was a legend, a true hero to some of us.

I was not there when this occurred, but my friend Mac was, and he's nothing if not a reliable source. This was 1962, when Mercy was fifteen and they were on a church trip to Ridgecrest Baptist Assembly in the North Carolina Smoky Mountains. Mac said that before they got out of town good, Mercy had lit a cigarette, thinking that sitting in the backseat behind the preacher with the windows down no one could smell the smoke. They were in the car with Brother Sims, the preacher, who said nothing about the smoking, though Mac said he tensed visibly every time Mercy lit up. They had left Rolling Fork in a caravan of six cars early that morning, and they were up well beyond Memphis when they decided it was time to stop for lunch. This was before fast food places, so they stopped at a little cafe in Jackson, Tennessee, for hamburgers and a rest. No sooner than they had finished the burgers and Cokes, Mercy went over to the jukebox and put a quarter in. The first song he played was Rufus Thomas' "Walking the Dog." You've got to remember that dancing was THE cardinal sin in the Baptist Church, with the preacher and deacons constantly trying to ban the high school dances after football games and even the prom. So Mercy started kind of shuffling by himself, scooting the chairs and tables around to make an impromptu dance floor, and walked over to Linda Brown, a big-bosomed fourteen year old, and pulled her onto the floor and began dancing, but not just dancing. Mac reported that Mercy would get up behind Linda and hump at her backside, all the while grinning and looking leeringly at them. The preacher was too shocked or scared to say anything, so while Linda bounced happily away, unaware of what was going on behind her, Mercy gyrated and humped and rubbed his hands on his own butt to the strains of Rufus Thomas. As soon as the song ended, Brother Sims wrangled everyone into the cars and they continued their journey. Mac said it was a long ride to Ridgecrest, with Brother Sims fuming the whole way while Mercy sat in the back smoking Lucky Strike after Lucky Strike. On their second day at the camp the administrators asked Mercy to leave, something to do with smoking, dancing and going around to the girl's cabins after dark, so they put him on a bus back to Rolling Fork. That only added to his esteem in our eyes.

I had asked about Mercy over the years, but no one had but the vaguest news of him. Everyone would say, "You know, he married some colored woman up north and is scared to come home. Broke his mama's heart." But I knew Mercy wasn't afraid of anyone, and I knew his mother loved him and his wife and their kids. I saw Brother Sims at the grocery the other day, and as we were talking he mentioned that Mercy had come to visit him the year before. It seems that he had gotten religion and felt that he owed Brother Sims an apology for his youthful indiscretions. That kind of made me sad. I never thought of Mercy as doing anything exactly wrong, just doing it his way. He was the product, as I was, of long afternoons of hanging around at the ice house and in the fields with ne'er-do-wells, storytellers, bullshitters, easy riders, and small-time con men. I guess if that's your truth, your life's experience, then what could be the problem?

What I wouldn't give today for a video of Mercy dancing in that cafe with Linda Brown in 1962. It may not be as good as the movie that plays in my mind when I think of it, but damn, I'd love to see that. Have Mercy!

The Anomaly of the Delta

China Street, Rolling Fork, Mississippi, 2009

In the past twenty or so years I've talked a lot about the Delta. I've written scripts for films, dozens of text panels for museums, books about Blues and cotton culture. I've interviewed hundreds of people about some aspect of southern culture or agricultural technology or art, and been invited to participate in panel discussions on the why and how of the Delta. I think the one revelation I have come to after these many, many hours and days and weeks of thinking about the place where I was born and raised, is the fact that it ever worked at all. The question usually has something to do with the Delta of ruin, the Delta of yesterday, the Delta of legend, the Delta of nostalgia. Maybe the decline of the diverse culture and small town atmosphere in the Delta is not the story. That so many unique elements came together at one time is the real story, and, hence, the anomaly.

The fact that the Yazoo-Mississippi River Delta was not inhabited in any great measure until around the turn of the twentieth century, and then by arguably the most eclectic and diverse group of immigrants, ne'er do wells, ex-enslaved, second sons of wealthy families, and wandering souls who were just looking to catch some traction somewhere, is the real story. Had it not been for the 'second slavery' or 'sharecropping' as they rechristened it, none of this would have ever come about. There are a few inflection points, most notably just after the civil war, then at the end of the Reconstruction debacle, next during the 1890s thru the early teens when the civil war conveniently got rewritten and the newly minted myth was roundly embraced by whites in the South, or after WWI, when Black soldiers returning from Europe were faced with renewed discrimination, or after WWII, when, again, African-Americans helped to win the war and came home to a country where they had no voice, no vote, no opportunity, and no prospects. Who knows how better their lives would have been in the North or in the West? The sad fact is that it wasn't until the mid 1960s that Delta African-Americans were dismissed, finally thrown away when the cotton picker and herbicides took away the only reasons, in the minds of their oppressors, for Blacks to be in the Delta at all: to chop and pick cotton, and to cook and housekeep for white families. Nevermind the decades of familial ties to that crescent of land. No thought of the contributions and unrealized potential of the majority of people who lived there. It is a sad, missed opportunity, yet that doesn't even approach the gravity of the situation.

When I was a kid in the 1950s and 60s, every one of those little Delta towns ran on what I call the $3-a-day economy. You chop cotton from early June till the crops are laid-by in mid- July. You make $3 a day. 7 in the morning till 6 in the evening. Five days a week, half-day on Saturday. Half hour for whatever lunch you brought that day. Everybody drinks out of the dipper and the five-gallon galvanized bucket. It might even have a little ice in it. Fifty or sixty people in the field, kids, mamas, grandmas. Old men who can't work much anymore are the keepers of the file, and will sharpen your hoe when you need it. The rows are sometimes a mile long, the sun hot, the dust deep, so you slide your bare feet along under the coolness of the dust. Not much singing going on in the fields, much to the chagrin of the ethnomusicologists who like to paint an alternate picture. No coded song lyrics or field hollers about the 'man.' Just groups of friends and neighbors working along, talking about what people talk about. Come Saturday at dinner time (lunch for those of you not from the South), they pay off and every person takes their little bit and spends it uptown in Rolling Fork. Groceries, cornmeal and flour, neckbones, lard, maybe some jaw breakers or two-for-a-penny cookies from the store, marbles and plastic toys, hair pomade, stockings, new pair of shoes, a straw hat, a new Sunday outfit, maybe even the picture show. All spent in a three or four block area where the streets are still crowded at 10 o'clock on Saturday night. The cafes where the jukebox thumps and smoked sausage sandwiches and quarts of beer are relished, pushing on through the night, providing the only respite from a life that is harder than any of you can imagine. And fights. Why, somebody would put a knot on your head if you looked at them wrong or said something stupid. In the juke joints an ice pick or straight razor was the weapon of choice.

The storekeepers knew that this was the time to make money, get all you could from these newly wealthy people. It wouldn't last long, six or eight weeks, but the influx of money was as good as at

Christmastime. The cotton picking money ran out by the mid 60s, when most farmers in the Delta had a mechanical picker, and the chopping money died a rapid death when the US Congress passed the Minimum Wage for Agricultural Workers bill, which in 1965 was $1 per hour. The $3 a day economy was dead, and within a couple of years, the small towns in the Delta began a slow and painful death that has lasted more than fifty years. The stores on China Street in Rolling Fork closed one by one. The last was Sam Sing and Company in 2015, the last of the four Chinese-owned grocery stores that gave the main drag in Rolling Fork its name. But before that Mr. Sam Rosenthal's dry goods store closed, then his sister's store, The Price-Rite Store, closed its pink doors, and Danzig's Furniture and Lamensdorf's weren't far behind. Mr. Denton closed the Five and Dime Store in the 80s, and Atchley's Rexall moved out to the highway where there was thought to be more traffic, and then closed as well. Most of the grocery stores had long since closed. All the little stores and shops were gone by the early 90s. Most downtown areas are now abandoned, and only chain stores like Dollar General or Family Dollar are left out on the highway to chew the last bits of commerce out of the communities.

When the growing and harvesting cotton demanded great numbers of people, the Delta thrived. Mechanization certainly improved farming techniques and the agricultural economy, but in the end it exacted a huge toll in human capital. It is estimated that over 6 million African Americans fled the rural South between 1910 and 1970, with 2.4 million leaving in the 1960s. As the northern cities where many of these migrants settled began to de-industrialize, and manufacturing jobs moved off-shore, opportunities were hard to come by, and great numbers of people fell into poverty. This time though, it wasn't just Black people. It was the working-class former union workers who got talked into voting against the union, or settling for a lopsided contract, or not complaining loud enough when those corporations they had relied on for generations simply locked the doors and moved away. No retraining, no penalties. The only people who won and continue to win are the stockholders in those companies who don't care how much the industries have to hop to the next poor society to keep those profit margins healthy. All of a sudden, Ohio, West Virginia, and Michigan look a lot like 1960s Mississippi.

The Delta was built on exploitation. Strike that. America was built on exploitation. Strike that. The world was built on exploitation, but that subject is much too simple or complex for me to deal with here. When I think about my place, the Mississippi Delta, it's clear that the task of "taming" a swampy, heavily forested region that runs some two hundred miles in length and eighty miles at its widest was a near impossible endeavor taken as a whole. The determination of those early settlers, and the methodical encroachment of one tree at a time, one load of timber at a time, one stump at a time, one field at a time, added up to the man-made, mechanical agricultural domain we see today.

A problem that persists to this day is that the Delta is a very insulated place. Very few "new" people come to settle and work among us. This wasn't the case in the beginning when immigrants from all over the western world were enticed with promises of jobs, good homes and fair wages. In reality, there were already quite enough people to do the work, but I'm convinced that the people in charge would have been okay with running all the Blacks out and replacing them with Italians, or Chinese, or Syrians, whom they looked upon as not technically white, but certainly closer than African Americans. My guess is that they figured they could get more work out of these new immigrants and they would be more pliable and reasonable. With ethnic group after ethnic group, the ploy didn't work. After a season of working a cotton crop these folks did whatever they could to set up businesses, most times to do business with Black people. The Italians ran cafes and got a toe-hold on the bootlegging and later the legal liquor store business, the Syrians started as peddlers and quickly became shopkeepers, the

Jewish saw a niche and went from selling rags out of a cart to owning dry goods stores all over the Delta, and the Chinese settled in as grocers. Anything but working in the cotton fields.

World War II changed the racial dynamic in America. Racial attitudes were changing, and a new type of segregation was on the rise. At the end of World War II, African Americans were faced with the new reality of ethnic groups such as Italians, the Jewish, Greeks, and others who had previously not been viewed as "white," becoming legitimized and welcomed into the mainstream of American life. At the same time, new Jim Crow laws and ever-strengthening opposition to the acceptance of Black people to share in the American dream was the new order of the day. The war, which many hoped would finally cause America to grant true equality to all, was a step backward for the African-American community.

My problem was trying to square the fact that so many people were okay that their fellow human beings were, for the most part, locked in this horrific daily struggle for survival. Somehow, we normalized it.

Where I grew up, to see some of the worst poverty on the planet one simply had to look out the window or walk down a street. Black children dressed in rags, an inordinate number of umbilical hernias on little kids, women hauling five gallon buckets of water from a common spigot down the way, all within sight of some of the most conspicuous consumption you can imagine. It's still that way, though many African Americans have figured out how to navigate the reality of the system and share in the bounty. Education and the vote have been the means to a better life. The recognition that with a little organization and cooperation most Delta counties could be run by African Americans, from sheriff to tax collector, to supervisor, to school board, thereby setting the course and reaping the benefits from state and federal government programs. It's still a struggle when the state legislature won't accept federal monies due to some vague principle that generally has its genesis in conservative church doctrine or in the belief that the entire country is out to get Mississippi. Will it ever change? Who knows? I do know this, the country is not thinking about Mississippi, at least not in that way. I think the people who run things will continue to shoot themselves in the foot at every opportunity.

Coach Grayson Plots My Future

It was a rite of passage, the meeting in the spring of your senior year with the guidance counselor. The world was changing, and the student was stepping onto a much bigger stage than tiny Rolling Fork, Mississippi. This was one of those meetings where it was rumored that the adult treated you like an adult, and talked with candor and insight. It seemed as though they, every teacher, coach, and even cafeteria workers, had watched your development as a human being, patiently for twelve years, guiding with a stern or compassionate hand, and this meeting was the culmination of it all.

Coach Grayson shook my hand when I entered the tiny office and offered a chair. We were sitting no more than three feet from one another. He leaned back and smiled a big, genuine smile.

"Dadgummit, you've come a long way, especially in this last year. Your grades are the best they've ever been, and I hear the deacons at the Baptist church came to see you about going to Mississippi College. What do you think?"

"Coach, I don't know. They want me to study the ministry, but I just don't feel called." I said this because it was exactly what the deacons heard when they came over to Dot's house the week after making the offer of paying for my tuition, room and board at Mississippi College, the Baptist institution in Clinton. They had come to supper the week before that, and afterwards we sat in the living room and they offered me the "chance of a lifetime" to be educated in the ministry. They had been impressed by my leadership skills among the other students. I'll admit, I had grown that year and a half I had lived in the tiny deep freeze room at the back of Dot's rambling house. The room was literally where the deep freezer had been till she got an upright and moved it into the kitchen. Folks in the Delta relied on freezers back then. It seemed that everyone had a garden or at least a friend with a garden, and the purple hull peas, lady peas, butter beans, tomatoes, squash, and okra flowed like manna from heaven from June through August. We shelled peas and beans till our thumbs were permanently stained purple. We ate the last of the previous year's crop and filled the freezer with plastic bags sized perfectly for the number of people in our family, and felt a sense of comfort knowing that whatever else happened, we'd be able to eat throughout the next year.

My choice was to live in this 4 ft. by 8 ft. room when I moved back from North Carolina, and I had outfitted it with a single bed, a bookcase filled with my collection of books that reached back to the moment a few years before when my mother discovered I didn't know how to read, and up until the present. There was an eclectic roadmap of my progress as a reader. The young reader hot rod books by Henry Gregor Felsen, trashy Southern novels by Lance Horner and Kyle Onstott, John Steinbeck novels, biographies of RFK, Tom Hayden, the Students for a Democratic Society (you see where we're going here), poetry by Lawrence Ferlinghetti, and Allen Ginsberg, and lastly, the novels of William Faulkner. Much of this consumption was due to Dot having a rule that we all went to bed at 9 pm. I was never sleepy at that time, so I read each night till midnight or later, and as a result I changed my life. My self-education was completely different from what they were teaching us at Fielding L. Wright Attendance Center just across the creek.

More importantly, the anxiety I had lived with of never knowing what was going to happen next was slowly receding as my new reality took shape. Living in Rolling Fork in a home that was not my own, being separated, by choice, from my family, while building a future that reflected very little on where I was or who I was at that moment was a revelation. I was fiercely preparing for a rich life I could neither articulate nor envision

When Coach Grayson offered advice on my future I was stunned. He said something like, "You know, Jimmy Blankenship really likes you, and told me he'd like for you to consider staying here in Rolling Fork and driving a truck for him. You know, he's got a growing business and you might fit right in. Folks are using a lot more chemicals these days, and it looks like that's the coming trend in farming. What do you think?"

What? Drive a truck? Don't you know that I'm a poet? I quit listening at that point and nodded politely till he let me go back to study hall. Years later, I would see Coach Grayson from time to time, and he would always shake my hand and hold onto it and look me in the eye and say, "I always knew you were going to do something special, something unique." I realized that that day, so long ago, he was gently pushing my buttons, knowing there was more to my story than staying in Rolling Fork and driving a truck. Just like me, he couldn't see what it was or what it even felt like, but he knew there was something different for me. I love that man for giving me his best. It took me years to realize it, but in his own way he could see my future.

A couple of days after I had the meeting with Coach Grayson, I got a call from the hospital in Belzoni. A doctor told me my father had fallen in a grocery store and broken his hip and cut his arm badly. The doctor told me he would probably be in the hospital for a week or two and then have to go to a rehab center till he could walk on his hip. This was long before hip replacement surgery, and many times a broken hip began the slow descent into death. He was only forty nine years old, but I was scared for him.

I remember being afraid to talk plainly to the doctor, but I knew things were certain to go badly within a couple of days if I didn't. I blurted out, "He's an alcoholic, and he needs a drink every few hours or he'll go into DTs." There was silence on the other end of the phone. I heard him sigh, and he said, "We are not in the business of giving whiskey to our patients. Maybe he needs to stop drinking." I thought about my conversation with Coach Grayson, and decided that for once I was going to speak to this adult as an equal.

"Look, he's going to go into DTs if he doesn't have a drink. Can you at least give him a beer every few hours? He's been in Whitfield before, and they gave him shock treatments. I'm not fooling. He's an alcoholic."

"Son, you're gonna have to let me be the doctor."

Two days later the same doctor called late in the afternoon. He was agitated. He told me that my father was hallucinating, and had tried to escape from his hospital room, but couldn't stand up on his broken hip. The stitches in his arm had opened and they found a big shard of glass from a broken Coke bottle still in his arm. He asked me what I was going to do.

"Send him to Whitfield," I said, and when I hung up the phone a minute later, I went back to my little room and sat for a long time. I was alone. My family was scattered to the wind, Jeff in the Coast Guard in Connecticut, Gaines in Arizona, Mama in North Carolina, and I was left to do the ugly job nobody else wanted or deserved to deal with.

Saturday, I borrowed Dot's '65 Bonneville and drove over to Whitfield, which was just outside Jackson. I waited in a small waiting room till the doctor could see me. He turned out to be a nice man who knew of my father's previous stay in the state mental hospital. As he flipped through a file folder, he told me they had gotten him calmed down and it looked like everything was going to work out with the hip and the gash on his arm. He closed the folder and looked at me for a few seconds. "What are you going to do with your father when he gets out?"

I didn't know what to say. He clearly was expecting me to have an answer or some kind of plan to deal with my father when it came time to discharge him from the hospital. I hadn't considered this, and I calmly told him, "Look, I'm graduating from high school next week. I've been living with a sort of relative for the past year and a half, so I really don't have anywhere to go myself. I think he's enough of a man to figure it out for himself. Maybe he can go back to Belzoni. He has some brothers and sisters in Port Gibson, maybe they can take care of him."

They wouldn't let me see him that day. To be honest, I didn't want to see him at all.

High School Graduate

The Graduate, Rolling Fork High School, 1969

It was late May in 1969, and my high school graduation was coming fast. Too fast. My parents were driving from North Carolina to celebrate the happy day with me and see me off on my next chapter in life. The last fourteen months had been a time of peace for me. Living in the deep freeze room was nothing short of a godsend. It was the home of my new stepfather's first cousin, who also happened to be my mother's best friend, Dot. She had introduced my mom and Joe in the summer of 1967, and by Christmas they were married.

I had spent six weeks in North Carolina with them in early 1968. My new school had over a thousand students in three grades. My school in Rolling Fork had just under six hundred students in grades one through twelve, kids I had been classmates with since I was five. The North Carolina school was so foreign to me. Kids talked and dressed differently, they listened to Carolina Beach Music, and danced like kids from the 1950s. It wasn't bad, just different, and not inviting. I was a nobody but I had once been a somebody. That's a hard place to be when you're 17.

My first day of school I met another kid who had just moved to the area from Kenya. His dad was a scientist for the U.S. Department of Agriculture, and had spent the past four years helping farmers in East Africa. Paul and I got to be fast friends, and within a week, we were skipping school school on the regular, listening to Jimi Hendrix records in his house or going to the beach and sitting for hours in the cold wind smoking cigarettes. Pretty soon we weren't going to school at all.

I knew I had to get out of there quickly, so I called Dot, who had told me when I was leaving that if I ever wanted to come back I could stay with her and finish the rest of 11th grade and my senior year. Through many phone calls, not a few tears, and some delicate diplomacy on my part, my mother relented and let me go back to the Delta.

I know six weeks isn't a long time, but it had broadened my worldview. I felt different when I got back. I didn't have as much patience with my old friends and began a slow but steady move away from the more dangerous and criminal leaners. The principal, Mr. Mullins, asked me several times when my grades would arrive from the NC school. I knew there weren't any grades, or certainly no passing grades, so I lied and put him off till he either forgot about it or got tired of asking me. Throughout the next year, he asked me a few times about the incomplete grades, but I pleaded innocence and promised I would get my mother to look into the issue. The situation is currently unresolved.

There was another problem looming on the horizon. I had failed algebra twice, once in the ninth grade and then again in the tenth. I had no interest in algebra. I still have no interest in algebra. I have never felt the need to know anything about algebra, but it seemed the state of Mississippi needed me to be proficient enough in it to at least squeak by with a D-, and thus have a well-rounded education. This was a problem. I needed to have two math credits to graduate. I had taken general math and somehow passed, but at the beginning of my senior year, Principal Mullins called me in his office and announced that I would have to take a correspondence course in algebra. This, frankly, seemed to be the answer to my prayers. I would get my math-smart friends to do my homework, and I would mail off the work to Mississippi Southern College in Hattiesburg for some math student to grade. Life was looking lovely.

I've still never read it.

April came, and Mullins asked when I was going to be finished with the course. I told him I thought I'd be done by May 1, and he said something to me that almost made me faint. "Well, good. I'll have the exam sent to me and you can take it in my office." EXAM? Nobody said anything about any exam. There was no way I could pass an algebra exam. I was doomed. I walked around in a fog for days, my mind racing from scenario to scenario, each coming back with the clear message that I was screwed. What would my mother think? What would Dot do to me? My whole world was about to come crashing down. Not graduating was unthinkable.

I successfully hid from Mullins for the next few weeks, but when he finally called me to his office, I was ready to break down and admit to everything, the lies, the obfuscation, the dilemma. I sat across from him, tears welling in my eyes, ready to finally get this thousand-pound weight off my shoulders. I had prayed, I had sworn that I'd never tell a lie again as long as I lived, I had bargained with God. Mullins shifted in his chair and leaned forward, his elbows on his desk, "Well, you've done it now," he said quietly.

I was just about to open the floodgates and admit to everything when he added, "Looks like you're going to have to drive all the way to Hattiesburg to take the exam. I talked with the folks down there and they're expecting you day after tomorrow."

Wait, what?

"Yeah, they had a bunch of kids from around the state who waited till the last minute to take the exam. He said it happens every year. They'll send me the grades a couple of days later. If you pass, you'll graduate."

I walked out of the office on a cloud. I have never been so relieved in my life. My first thought was to go to George, who was my best friend and the smartest guy in our class and ask him if he thought he could take the test for me. My bargaining and repentance flew out the window with blinding speed. George said it would be no problem, so we took off for Hattiesburg. I gave him my driver's license. Back then the Mississippi license was a piece of index card that had been filled out with a typewriter. It didn't matter that his eyes were blue and mine were brown. He waltzed into the exam building and appeared half an hour later, telling me that he "missed a couple" to make it look good. We got a good chuckle about that.

As much as I was feeling that I had dodged a bullet, I still felt some anxiety that something might happen to derail what looked to be my hard-fought victory. Once again, I found Jesus.

The baccalaureate was scheduled for Sunday evening. Graduation was set for the next Friday night. The fifty four of us were in the auditorium practicing the march down the aisles, the piano beating out "Pomp and Circumstance," listening to our teachers go over the rules of deportment, how we should dress, and how to turn in our caps and gowns. Suddenly, Mullins appeared at the door. He immediately made eye contact with me. My heart sank. My stomach turned. I got hot all over. He walked in, still eyeing me, and announced, "I have some interesting news." Oh, shit. I tried not to look at George. If we got caught, they might not let him graduate. I suddenly felt so reckless and selfish. If I were the cause of him not being able to attend Washington & Lee, I would never forgive myself. And my parents were to arrive later that day. These thoughts raced through my head. I began to see spots before me. I thought I might throw up.

Mullins got a big grin on his face, "I just got a call from Mississippi Southern and they told me that Willy made a 94 on his exam and passed with an A minus." The class applauded. I finally looked at George and he just nodded. I had made it.

Sometimes, early in the morning, when I'm between sleep and wakefulness, I wonder if I need to show up at Rolling Fork High School that day for any reason. And, let me say that fifty-four years later, George still has my back.

I Saw Elvis

Memphis bus station photo booth, 1972

I saw Elvis one time. I had come to Memphis in late December of '71 and moved in with a friend from the Delta who was living with this odd group of out-of-control Vietnam veterans who had turned into junkies and thieves. In fact, when I talked to my friend Arkansas on the phone about moving in, he had proudly announced that he was one of the biggest pot dealers in Memphis. That should have tipped me off as to what I was entering. We lived in a little house in a Black neighborhood. In the 1970s it was rare to find white people living in traditionally Black neighborhoods. No one ever messed with us, and for that matter they never spoke to us. I think the neighbors sized these old boys up in a hurry and decided to keep their distance. There was open drug dealing and stolen goods and cars and motorcycles and the occasional Hell's Angel on the front porch. The vets were some hard dudes as I remember. Drug-wise, they would take anything, anytime. I once saw one of them, a guy they called Gopher, shoot up heroin, then speed, then Nembutal, before passing out and foaming at the mouth. They thought he was dead, and he sure looked dead, but they were all laughing and kind of enjoying slapping him to get him back alive. They finally put him in the bathtub and put some more speed in his arm and he came back around. That was the kind of place it was. A friend visited me there one weekend and was scared out of his mind the entire time. It may have been due to the LSD he took on Saturday afternoon. He kept calling it a "transmission neighborhood," and kept asking me what my mother would think if she came to claim my body and saw the house and neighborhood.

I only stayed around for about two weeks, then my friend George came and rescued me and took me to the apartment where he and his girlfriend lived. Everything was pretty normal for the first couple of days till Arkansas showed up at midnight with his junkie girlfriend, Jilly, who looked kind of like Todd Rundgren, skinny and waif-like, but cute in an odd way. They stood at the door and begged George to let them sleep on the floor for the night, and George finally relented. We smoked a joint and everybody cooled out for a while, even laughing about some old times. We had only known one another for about two years at that point and here we were reminiscing about old times. It's even funnier now to think of those fragile and tenuous lines of friendship we fooled ourselves with back then. You could become someone's closest friend in less than a week, then they'd probably screw you over for something like a bag of weed, and you'd move on to someone else. I wonder if it was the times or just our youth?

The early 70s were a strange time when people in the South especially had just turned on and everything seemed new and exciting. We were a part of the revolution that had been going on all over America. Everyone had long hair and wore beads and leather and bellbottoms and talked about peace and being against the war and did drugs without a thought for the consequences. It was also a time of being the weirdest person you know and by that I mean that everyone, and I mean everyone, tried their damnedest to be freaky and weird and bizarre. I saw a film a few years ago that was made from some old footage shot by this guy back in the early 70s, and decades later edited by some younger guys. They thought they really had found some treasure trove of weirdness in this particular group of people. They kept saying, "Hell, who hung out with Hells Angels, and cowboys and hippies and bluesmen? This is some crazy shit!" But it wasn't crazy shit at all, it was pretty ordinary for the times when everyone was some kind of character and they played that character every day, wore the costume, and talked the talk. Maybe it was different on the west coast or in New York, but I kind of doubt it. Very few people had found their true direction, and even though this was pretty full of shit, it was at least different. Everyone was acting like a bizarre, bohemian, writer/sage/Leary-ite/Kerouac-quoter/fashion plate. A lot of these people still lived at home with their parents. The 60s happened in the 70s in the South.

So, later that night I was sleeping in the living room on a mattress in my army surplus sleeping bag, and Jilly and Arkansas were on another mattress in the dining room. Something woke me up and I looked across the room and couldn't see them. The room was filled with thick black smoke. I ran over, and just at that moment a flame sprang up by Jilly's head, and I could see her cigarette in the middle of a burned hole about the size of a salad plate in the mattress.

Smoke was pouring out of the hole and her hair was on fire. I reached down and grabbed her by the football jersey she slept in, picked her up, ran into the bathroom, and turned on the faucet in the bathtub, and put her head under the stream. She woke with a scream. I left her in the bathroom and went in and pushed Arkansas off the mattress and we dragged the mattress and half-burned foam rubber pillow out into the parking lot. We went back in and opened the doors and windows and hoped no one would call the fire department. George got thrown out of the apartment later that day.

George rescued me in 1972. We're still friends today.

Anyway, for the first couple of weeks I lived in Memphis, we lived near Graceland, where Elvis lived. Every morning and afternoon when we passed the Graceland gates there would be somewhere between ten and twenty people standing there, waiting for Elvis to come driving through, but mainly it would be his hangers-on, the Memphis Mafia, his daddy, or the dry cleaners or the maid coming to work. The fans stood there, waiting, thrilling at each car that rolled up or down the driveway, straining to see into the backseat to see if it was the King of Rock 'n Roll. I know this sounds cruel now, and it makes me a little embarrassed to even write it, but as we passed by in the VW bus every morning on our way to work at the glass factory, and then on our way home in the afternoon, I would yell out the back window, "Hey! He's in here with us!" and they'd all turn, looking intently for Elvis in the back of a VW microbus with a bunch of longhairs. My friends would look at me as we approached Graceland with the look of, *Please don't.* But I'd do it, just to keep my record consistent. Well, after about two weeks of these twice-a-day yellings, we approached Graceland on a Saturday afternoon. There were at least thirty fans at the gates. I yelled, they looked, my friends groaned. We got to the next traffic light and Charlie said in this almost reverent tone, "Oh, shit, look." Sitting on a motorcycle with a girl, right there beside us at the traffic light, was the King himself. My face burned with shame. My only thought was, "Damn, I hope he didn't hear me." The King looked over at us, nodded and gunned the three-wheeler down Elvis Presley Boulevard. I never yelled out the window at Graceland again, and even more importantly, looking at Elvis for those intense three seconds, he became a person to me, and I never wanted to joke about him again. It still makes me uncomfortable when I hear comedians making fun of Elvis.

Elvis on a motorcycle. (as artificial intelligence imagines him.)

Hitch Hiking

Denver Colorado, 1978. Photo by Charles Ray Perkins

I was the king hitchhiker. Between 1969 and 1975, I probably hitchhiked 25,000 miles. I would go anywhere and pretty much did. Once, I went to El Paso, Juarez, Albuquerque, Denver, around to Oklahoma City, and back to Memphis with no more than $14 in my pocket. Other times I would get a friend to give me a ride down to Southaven, just across the Mississippi line on I-55, to head south. Jackson, New Orleans, Rolling Fork, Hattiesburg, wherever the mood sent me. Hang out my thumb, look like an innocent college student, shoot the shit with whoever picked me up, and there I was, somewhere else. Turn around and go back home after the weekend. When I went to visit my parents on the coast of North Carolina I would take the overnight bus (if I had a little money) to Knoxville, get out on the highway and make my way over to the coast. On the way back I'd do the opposite, or sometimes my folks would take me to Raleigh and I'd hitchhike back to Memphis. I can still see the look on my mother's face when they would drive off. As a parent, I know that exact feeling. Obviously, times change (thanks Charles Manson), and the hitchhiking game went away. In the late 1960s, it was a viable and common way to get from one place to another.

I can't fathom how many cars I got into during that time. Hundreds. How I didn't get killed, I'll never know. Drunk drivers, crazy people, suspected serial killers, high school kids, criminals, preachers, pedophiles, tough guys, poor people, you name it, I rode with it.

About 80% of my rides were perfectly normal and forgettable, but the other twenty percent were epic. A few choice vignettes for my readers:

Two fraternity boys from Mississippi State picked me up one day. We drove along for a while till the guy in the passenger seat turned around and started telling me about this dude they had heard about who hitchhiked everywhere. He was known throughout the South as the best hitchhiker around. Just as I geared up to dismiss this pretender, the guy looked at me and said, "You ever heard of a guy named Willy Bearden?" I just about fainted right there in the backseat. It was a "Twilight Zone" moment if there ever was one. I hesitated and said in a quiet voice, "I'm Willy Bearden." I thought the driver was going to run off the road. He and the other guy were completely freaked out. After a few minutes, we figured out that they were in this fraternity with Roger Truesdale from Rolling Fork, who was and still is quite the raconteur. Roger had been bragging at the fraternity house about my hitchhiking around the country, and these guys were apparently in the business of spreading my legend.

A guy, who was mostly scared, robbed me of six dollars once. He reached under the driver's seat and pulled out a little .25 caliber pistol and pointed it at me while holding it in his lap. He wouldn't look at me. After I gave him the money (all I had was six crumpled dollars) I waited a minute and asked him to not point the gun at me. He pointed it at the floor and we rode in silence for another twenty minutes before he pulled to the side of I-55 and let me out at the Brooks Road exit in Memphis. I threw a rock at his car as he sped away.

I was hit on by more homosexuals than I can remember. I got so good at turning them down that I rarely offended any of them. The late sixties and early seventies in the South didn't see gay bars, gay newspapers, or gay hotels. Bus stations and maybe some bathrooms at rest areas provided the few opportunities available for gay travelers. A gay guy would pick me up and maybe give me a beer or two and make his play. I'd say something like, "Hey man, I'm not like that. If I was, we'd have a great time, but I'm not. That doesn't do anything for me, as you can understand. It would be like some woman trying to talk you into having sex with her. Now, that wouldn't be right, would it?" He'd think for a minute and say, "Are you sure?" and I'd say, "Yeah, I just don't think it would work," and we'd drive on.

In 1973, I rode from East Tennessee to Memphis with a van-load of junkies who stopped at stores along the way to shoplift. We drove around Jackson, Tennessee for over an hour looking for heroin. I kept telling them that I didn't think there would be any heroin in Jackson, but undeterred, they drove around aimlessly, stopping to talk with anyone with long hair. We finally made it to Memphis. About six months later I saw two of the guys hitchhiking on Poplar Avenue in Memphis. I didn't stop.

The last time I hitchhiked was in 1976. I had been living in Jackson, Mississippi with some friends. We had a band called The Columbus Flood Band. My friend Charlie and I hitched a ride to Memphis on a Sunday from a friend who had been in Jackson for the weekend, and I promptly came down with the flu. I was running a high temperature and feeling terrible. By Tuesday, I knew I needed to get back to Jackson. Charlie and I got a ride down to Southaven and stuck our thumbs out. We got a couple of rides and made it to Grenada without any problem, then we got picked up by some people in a white van. They slid the side door open, and we piled onto a mattress that took up most of the floor. There was a guy asleep on the mattress, a young woman holding a baby, sitting by him, a guy driving, and a girl in the front passenger seat. The girl with the baby was British and told us they were heading to Mardi Gras. We talked for a minute, and they said they would take us all the way to Jackson. Everything was going great. We were making small talk for a few minutes, and I was so relieved I wasn't standing out on the roadside. I was hoping to go to sleep and wake up when we got to Jackson. I was sitting as far back in the van as I could, trying to stay away from the girl and the baby and the guy sleeping on the mattress, when the guy rolled over and looked me in the face, then looked at Charlie and said, "Who're these muthafuckers?" I realized at that moment that he hadn't been sleeping. He had been passed out. The British girl's eyes got wide and she said, in the most perfect Marianne Faithful British accent I had ever heard, "Bobby, please! Please go back to sleep, you're pissed as a loon." The couple upfront laughed loudly. Bobby narrowed his eyes and started crawling, no, flailing, back to where I was huddled in the corner. He was swinging his arms wildly and saying, "I'm gonna kill these muthafuckers!" British girl was now screaming, "Bobby! Bobby! Bobby don't!" Charlie looked at me like he was ready to deck Bobby. Bobby rose to his knees, took a deep breath, and announced, "Pull over, I've got to piss." Bobby wasn't from England. His accent sounded distinctly southern Ohio or Indiana. He spun around, lost his balance, and was swimming on the mattress, trying to get back up. He finally gained some purchase and lunged between the front seats, laughing maniacally. He grabbed the steering wheel. Mind you, we're doing seventy-five or eighty, and he tried to pull the van off the road, all the while laughing and screaming, "I've got to take a piss!" The driver knocked his hand away and skidded to a stop on the right-hand shoulder. Cars were streaming by. Bobby crawled to the sliding door and opened it. With superhuman speed, he jumped out of the van, pulled his pants down to his ankles and was stumble-pissing all over himself and the roadside. We got out of the van and tried to help him stand, but he was having none of it. Stumbling, arms flailing. At this point, it quickly turned to a humanitarian rescue. This guy was all but naked on the side of Interstate 55, and he might've been an asshole, definitely was an asshole, but we couldn't leave this dude hanging like that. Charlie got around behind him and grabbed his arms. His driver buddy pulled his pants up and we wrestled him back in the van. Marianne Faithful has been steadily screaming, "Bobby, Bobby, please!" The girl in the passenger seat laughed herself purple. I think she was drunk, too. The driver thought it was all hilarious, as well. We threw Bobby in through the sliding door and we were off again. With his bladder freshly emptied, he was ready to fight again and started swinging at me. I say he was swinging, but in reality, he was flailing about in slow motion, landing a light tap every ten tries, so much so that I began thinking, "If he touches me again I'm going to knock a knot on his head." Charlie grabbed him and pulled him back onto the mattress. "Stop the car!" I screamed. "Stop the goddam car! Right now!" That seemed to get everyone's attention. "Pull over."

The driver was still laughing, "He's okay. He won't fuck with you anymore, will you, Bobby?"

Bobby was muttering to himself, but casting a wary eye at Charlie, who seemed to have had enough, too. Charlie said, "Stop the car and let us out, and I mean it." The tone of his voice let the driver guy know he wasn't kidding. The driver said, "Hey man, there's an exit a mile up the road, I'll let you off there." We rode the next minute in silence. As we were getting out, they were apologizing all over the place. "Dude, Bobby's a good guy, he's just drunk. He got started on Mardi Gras before we got to New Orleans. Look, we're gonna stop for gas, if you change your mind, just flag us down when we get back on the highway. We'll take you all the way to Jackson." As Charlie and I walked up the entrance ramp in the cold, he brought up the subject of getting back in the car with them. "No fucking way," I said. "That moron's gonna get somebody killed and it ain't gonna be me. I thought we were gonna wreck when he grabbed the wheel. Fuck him, we should have beat his ass right there on the side of the road."

A few minutes later the van turned onto the ramp and slowly made its way toward us. "You sure?" Charlie said.

"Yeah, I can't do it. I feel like shit, but I'm not going to fight that guy off for the next hour and a half."

Charlie waved them past us when they slowed down. The driver waved.

Even though it was only about 2 in the afternoon, it was getting cold. Mississippi can be brutal in the winter. We stood there for another twenty minutes or so, not talking. I was feeling worse and worse. All of a sudden a Mississippi Highway Patrol cruiser barreled up the ramp and stopped in front of us.

"Did you guys get out of a white van?"

"No," Charlie said, then looked at me to finish the lie.

I looked the trooper in the eye, "No sir, we got a ride with a man in an older Ford Falcon station wagon. It was green. He turned off here and said he was going into Winona. Older fella." My inner voice was screaming, "Shut up, you idiot! You're over-explaining. He's gonna know you're lying!"

"Well, we just got a call on the radio that three longhaired guys were beating up a nekkid man on the side of the road back there a few miles north. So, you haven't seen a white van pass by here?"

"Nossir, we just got dropped off at the bottom of the exit and walked up here a few minutes ago."

The trooper narrowed his eyes and said, "You do know it's against Mississippi law to be hitchhiking on this highway, don't you?"

"Yessir, we're just trying to get home to Jackson, and I've got the flu."

The radio in the car began squawking and the trooper got in and sped off.

"Oh, shit," Charlie shook his head, "if he catches up to that van they're gonna tell him we were riding with them. And they're probably gonna blame the whole thing on us. We better get a ride soon or he's gonna come back here and arrest us." The thought of spending a couple of days in the Winona, Mississippi jail scared me to death. We saw another state trooper heading north on the interstate. Things were heating up.

Just then, an older Plymouth pulled over a hundred yards or so ahead of where we were standing. Charlie looked at me and grinned, "Let's go, run!"

"Get in the back," the driver said. He looked to be about 16 years old. The girl sitting next to him looked to be the same age. The two girls in the backseat looked 14 or 15. The driver sped off and began telling us the story of their escape from some shithole town in Kentucky the night before. We were told that they had stolen a bottle of downers and they were all fucked up and headed to Mardi Gras. Within a few minutes, the driver was doing eighty. I noticed the tires were all but bald. That, for some reason, was something I always checked before I got into a car. I was sitting right behind the driver. He began to slowly run off the road. His chin was sitting on his chest and I saw that he was asleep. *ASLEEP!* I slapped him on the shoulder, and he woke up and swerved the car back into the lane.

"Hey man, let me drive," I said sternly.

"I'm okay. I can drive."

"Just let me drive. You can get back here and sleep for a few minutes."

"Hey man, what if *you* took three downers?"

"I don't know, but I know you've been driving for a long time and I just want you to be cool and get to New Orleans and have some fun."

He kept driving; I think he even sped up a little. The girl sitting beside me smiled through her druggy haze and I thought, "We would have been better off in the van with Bobby."

Five minutes later, as we were passing two cars, he fell asleep again. This time I whacked him good. We swerved into the other lane, somehow missed both cars and came to a stop off the shoulder of the road. We sat there for a few seconds.

"Okay, you can drive."

"Fuck you, man. Goddammit, you almost got us killed."

"You can drive."

"No, I'm getting out here."

Charlie said to me, "We're in the middle of nowhere."

"I don't care, you can ride with these morons. I'm getting out here."

They tried to talk us into getting back in the car, but I was done. I walked away from the car.

We walked for a couple of miles, still trying to hitchhike, but no one would pick us up. We finally got to a service station and called Carl in Jackson. He came and got us. I was sick with the flu for the next week. I never hitchhiked again.

On a lighter note, I did screw this girl who picked me up in Greenwood one day. She drove a white '59 Ford. I could tell she was about half drunk, so I asked if I could drive. A big ole raw-boned country gal, double jointed, as my friends would say. No one would describe her as pretty, but she was out for fun and had a pint of vodka.

She planned to meet her boyfriend at a rough joint over in Greenville called Tilley's, where every mean redneck in the Delta hung out. He had gotten off a riverboat that afternoon and looked forward to partying after having been out of circulation for thirty days.

I had long hair for 1969 and was regularly yelled at and even chased by rednecks like the ones we would soon encounter. As soon as I got into the driver's seat, she scooted up close to me and slid her dress way up above her knees till I could see her panties. By the time we were on the outskirts of Itta Bena, she was rubbing my leg and smiling a crooked smile as she sipped from the pint. She kept asking me, "What are you gonna do with this when we get to Greenville?"

I was game. I looked down and smiled at her, "Baby, I think we're gonna have a hell of a time when we get to Greenville. Are you sure you want to go to Tilley's though? That's a mighty rough place."

We stopped in Leland at a service station and asked where the liquor store was. Another pint took us to Greenville. It wasn't quite dark when we pulled up to Tilley's, so I parked in the back, under some trees. She had already crawled over into the backseat by the time I parked the Ford. I hoped to god that the boyfriend hadn't been looking out the door waiting for her. I would've been a dead man. I crawled into the backseat, and she cuddled up next to me. She gave me the sloppiest drunk kiss I've ever had. Nature and 19 year-old me took hold, and we were rolling around on the backseat. She started yelling, saying the nastiest things I had heard up to that moment in my life, and I realized I had made a big mistake.

"Hey, we better be a little quieter, you don't want your boyfriend to hear us, do you?"

"I don't like that bastard anyway. He just uses me for my money and my car, and maybe my kitty. I like you now. Come on."

"Yeah, I like you too, but if he's waiting for you there might be trouble, and I'm a lover, not a fighter."

"That skinny little bastard couldn't whip your ass on a good day. Anyway, I'd help you." She thought for a second. "He does carry a switchblade though and went to jail for cutting this old boy."

"Parchman?"

"No, just the county jail up there in Grenada."

"OK. How bad did he cut him?"

"He didn't stab him or nothing. He just cut his arm and a little on his stomach. Don't stop!"

"OK, I won't, but you're gonna have to be a little quieter, folks are gonna be parking here in a minute."

We lay there, both out of breath. She said, "Where we goin' now?"

"I thought you were gonna pick up your boyfriend and go back to Grenada."

"I changed my mind."

"Well, you don't want to leave him high and dry, do you? Thirty days is a long time out on that riverboat."

"I don't care nothin' about him."

"Look, I've got to get to Rolling Fork. Uh, my uncle Bobby died, and I have to be a pallbearer tomorrow. How about I get up with you in Grenada on Sunday?" All this said while I was pulling on my pants and opening the door. I had a bad feeling I would have to face some hard-ass skinny dude with a switchblade if I tarried. I leaned down to the window.

"I guess I'll give that son-of-a-bitch a ride home," she said, pulling her dress over her head. "Come here and give me some sugar."

I kissed her and started to make my way out of the parking lot, walking fast. Cars were streaming in, and I knew I was in the wrong place, or maybe the right place, for an ass-whipping.

"Hey!" she yelled across the gravel parking lot, "What's your name?"

"Sonny."

"Hey, you want to take the pint?"

"Naw, you keep it."

"OK, Sonny from Rolling Fork. I'll see you Sunday. Be at that ham store out by the highway. You know that store, don't you?"

I didn't keep our Sunday afternoon rendezvous. After all, how could I find her in Grenada? I didn't even know her name.

Some months later I was sitting in the pool hall when Johnny B., who worked at Ed Davis' service station out on the highway, walked by and motioned for me to come outside, since no Black people were allowed inside the pool hall. He told me a white woman had been by looking for me. He said when he was filling up the car with gas, she whispered to him and asked about a long-haired hitchhiker named Sonny from Rolling Fork. Though he knew exactly who she was talking about, he said that didn't ring a bell, and maybe she meant Rosedale or Ruleville. She said she was sure it was Rolling Fork.

"Johnny, what kind of car was she driving?"

"It was a old white Ford, burning as much oil as it was gas. Had a little ole weaselly lookin' white mane with her."

"Hmm, ain't no tellin' who she was lookin' for."

He winked, "Yeah, ain't no tellin."

After that, every time I saw Johnny B., he winked and called me a "mannish boy." Not a bad reputation to have with the Black folks around Rolling Fork.

In 1973, I hitchhiked from Memphis to Jackson, Mississippi to visit a friend at Millsaps College. It was a beautiful Friday fall afternoon, and I looked forward to going somewhere. Halfway down I-55 to Jackson, a girl picked me up in what we'd now call an SUV, but you didn't see them much then. It was some GMC or Chevrolet thing. She had long, curly, Carole King hair, and a look that pierced my soul. We talked and talked. I think she was a couple of years older than me, or at the very least, more mature. She was one of the most beautiful women I had ever seen. I did my best to charm her. When she looked at me, she was looking right into my soul. I longed for a hippie girl like this. She exited the highway and delivered me to the front of my friend's fraternity house. We sat in the car, neither of us wanting to say goodbye, but my buddy and his friends came out of the house on their way to getting drunk. They strode to where we sat and welcomed me with a big joint. I started to tell them that I couldn't stay because I really wanted to go on to New Orleans with this girl, but something made me take my backpack out of the backseat and tell her goodbye. The moment she pulled away I knew my mistake. Here was a chance to change my life forever, and I had blown it. I saw her look up to the rearview mirror as she drove away.

Why was I always looking for someone to save me? Or maybe not save me, but certainly change the trajectory of my life. I seemed to be looking for some abrupt changing-of-the-channel moment to take me away from my reality and welcome me to the path I was truly meant to travel. Delusional? Probably. Young and naive? Definitely.

Another thing happened on that trip. After my friend presented me with the freshly-rolled joint, he announced we were going to see his girlfriend in a performance of Noel Coward's "The Importance of Being Earnest." So, an hour and a half later I found myself standing in the auditorium at Millsaps College looking for a place to sit for the next couple of hours. I walked toward the stage and saw an older woman sitting by herself on the third or fourth row. I instantly recognized her as Eudora Welty. I stood there for another minute or two to see if anyone was going to sit with her. I made my move.

"Excuse me, Miss Welty, but is anyone sitting here?" I nodded to the empty seat next to her.

She smiled, "Why, no, would you like to join me?"

"Yes ma'am. I'm Willy Bearden from Rolling Fork, but I live in Memphis now."

"Well, Willy Bearden from Rolling Fork, have a seat."

I was sitting with Eudora Welty. I first read her story "Petrified Man" when I was 16. I remember thinking that she somehow must have read my mind about what goes on in the beauty shop. I was stunned by how she had captured the essence of that hallowed place. The voices leaped from the page and sat in my ear like a favorite song. I remember having the revelation that the beauty shop was an important place. Then I saw that her story had been written in 1939, and I knew that writing like this was timeless. She had lifted the everyday, the commonplace, to great heights in my mind. This may have been the first time I had an inkling that I had something to say, something to contribute.

We had a little small talk about Rolling Fork. She seemed to remember some folks from there. Then my friend came and sat beside me. He was clearly impressed that I had been so bold as to sit by the great woman. He leaned and whispered to me, "Ask her what her fantasies are."

The curtain rose and the play began. At the intermission we talked about the play and she said the Millsaps Theater productions were one of her favorite things to see. She was easy in her conversation, asking about what I did in Memphis and where I worked. When the play was over my friend headed backstage to congratulate his girlfriend. Miss Welty and I sat there till the crowd thinned out, and I walked her out to her car.

I don't live with many regrets, but I see now that had I written to Miss Welty the next week I believe we would have had a long friendship. There is some quizzical paradox in the two very consequential things that happened to me that day in 1972.

Uncle Billy's Tattoos

You really have to be careful when considering a tattoo. I once dated this girl from Belzoni, Mississippi who had this crazy uncle who had tattooed what appeared to be random letters on the fingers of both hands. Random, that is, until he laced his fingers together, and there, as if by magic, it spelled out

"Let's Fuck." This was his standard honky tonk come-on, and he came to know if the woman laughed, he was getting laid. This guy was a little scrawny alcoholic who loved to fight men, women, and even kids when he got drunk, which was pretty much every day of his life. He had been married five times, the longest lasting just over a year, and the shortest...six days. His face was a mess of scars, and his nose had been flattened so many times he looked like a down-on-his-luck boxer, which I kind of guess is what he was. He was a pretty good guy but you never knew what was going to set him off, so you were always on pins and needles just waiting for what you were sure was going to come. I saw him get into an argument with a guy over pickled eggs one day. I was giving him a ride to his niece's (my girlfriend's) house, and of course he wanted to stop by a country store for a cold beer. No sooner than he walked to the counter to pay for the beer (he was a dedicated Falstaff man), the man behind the counter asked if he wanted a pickled egg. Billy Paul, that was his name, took a step back and said to the man, "And just what the fuck would I want with one of them goddam pickled eggs? You think I don't eat nothin' but n****r food?"

The man stammered some apology, saying that lots of folks enjoyed the eggs with their beer, and that he didn't mean any harm.

Well, that really set Billy off. "So you think I'm some kind of goddam alcoholic? Is that what you think? Fuck you and the goddam horse you rode in here on." And with that he raked his arm across the counter and pushed the whole gallon jar of eggs off onto the floor with a tremendous crash. The immediate stink of vinegar and boiled eggs filled the room.

The man reached under the counter, I think for a pistol, and I grabbed Billy Paul's arm and dragged him out of the store and into the car, him cussin' a blue streak and trying to take a swing at me the whole way, saying he was going to whip somebody's ass. We drove off in a hail of thrown gravel from my spinning tires, Billy Paul hanging out the window yelling that he'd be back and he'd have his goddam gun too. "Son of a bitch don't think I got me a gun, does he? I'll show his ass something. Take me back to the house." And on and on till I finally got rid of him by driving off after I had promised I'd wait at his house till he got his pistol and we'd go back to the store and "straighten that motherfucker out once and for all". I knew I'd pay for it the next time I saw him, but I couldn't put up with his bullshit, no matter how cute Kathy (his niece) was. And she was heartbreakingly cute. We broke up pretty soon after, and I was kind of relieved, knowing that I wouldn't have Billy in my life for the next forty years, spoiling every Christmas, every fish fry, every family reunion with some crazy fistfight or cussing someone out for no good reason. The funny thing is, I kind of liked him, and I felt terrible when I heard, about ten years later that Billy had been in an accident and had lost his left arm, so now all he had was the letters: L T S F C on the fingers of his right hand. He had gone to sleep, drunk of course, at a boat dock where he was working, and the little train track mechanism they used to slide boats down the hill into the water had caught his arm and ripped nearly it off. The arm couldn't be saved. I never asked what they did with the ruined arm. Maybe they buried it.

When I was younger I always worried that my friends wouldn't mesh. I was hesitant to ever have a party when I lived in Memphis because I knew so many people from different worlds, and I could never imagine them liking one another or having anything to talk about. I was scared my Mississippi friends would somehow embarrass me by saying racist things, or that my musician friends would talk about drugs to my older, settled, married friends from the neighborhood. I probably missed some real creative opportunities, not to mention great stories, by not letting these groups mingle in the free-for-all that I understand today is just life. It was the desire to control things and make sure that no one was ever offended, no one was diminished in any way, that ruled my life for so many years. I don't feel that way anymore.

James, 1972

James was this guy I knew from T&F Liquors. T&F stood for Trigg and Florida, a rough neighborhood store in a rough part of South Memphis. The 1960s had not been kind to South Memphis, and James was like a lot of guys whose lives orbited the parking lot around the liquor store. There was usually a dice game going on in the back parking lot, and fights were a regular thing with the men and women who hung out there. I watched my back when I was delivering to T&F and another store over on Lauderdale, where the owner walked me in with a sawed off 12 gauge the first time I delivered there. Memphis was rough back in the early 70s.

Anyway, James was one of the day-labor guys I could count on to help unload a boxcar or a semi trailer of whiskey or wine. I'd go over early in the morning and find a couple of guys who wanted to work, then take them back late in the afternoon. James and I got to be friends when we were unloading a boxcar full of Jack Daniel half pints. I shared my lunch with him that first day, and that earned me respect in his eyes. Later, we were sitting in the door taking a cigarette break when suddenly James leapt out of the boxcar and scurried around on the ground like a crazy man.

"What in the hell are you doing, man?" I seriously thought he had lost his mind.

"Got dam! Got dam!" he hollered, and stood up holding a toad.

"What the hell are you doing with that frog? He's gonna piss on you and give you warts."

"Mane, shit," he laughed, "we got it made now."

"What?"

"I done found this lucky frog. Reckon can we go to the dog track tonight? I'll give you a dollar for gas." He held the frog up for me to see.

"Man, I don't have a car."

"See can't we take one of the trucks?"

"Man, are you crazy? We can't take the liquor truck to the dog track. Why do you want to go anyway?"

"Look." He turned the frog over, and right there under its wide mouth, in the middle of a cream colored patch of flesh was a perfect 7.

"Ain't every frog got a number, so when you finds one you know it's good luck. My cousin found one with a 4, and he won 92 dollars at the dog track." He put the toad down gently and watched as it hopped away.

"Oh, bullshit. I don't believe that." I flicked my cigarette as James climbed back into the boxcar.

"You finna pass up a golden opportunity that don't come along every day," he eyed me seriously, "Can't you borrow one of your friends' cars? Look here, I'll split the money with you. We can get our checks cashed at the dog track, drink a coupla beers, eat a hotdog, and come home with some money."

"Alright, I'll see. Maybe Carl will take us over there."

"I ain't splittin' my money with him. I don't know no Carl." James crossed his arms and looked at me hard.

"I'm not asking you to split anything. We don't even need to tell him about the frog if you don't want to."

"I DON'T want to. Let's give him a dollar's worth of gas and see cain't he take us."

On through the afternoon we worked and finally unloaded the last case of half-pints out of the boxcar. I drove him back over to the T&F parking lot, and we made plans to meet there at 7 that night to go to West Memphis.

I talked Carl into giving us a ride by promising I'd buy him all the beer he could drink. We pulled into the T&F parking lot and sure enough, James was waiting. He came up to the car window and told me he wouldn't be able to go that night because his plans had changed. I got out of the car and said, "Hey man, what about the lucky frog? We talked about this shit all day, are you sure?"

"Yeah, man, I ain't going to be able to go. Something else came up."

I knew that fucker had found another ride to the dog track when he had second thoughts about splitting his winnings with me. He already had that money spent. I was kind of pissed, but a little relieved too. I could see that James wasn't the most reliable cat, and who knew what might transpire when he got a few beers into the evening.

"Hey, no big deal, man."

"Alright, I'll see you next week," he walked away.

The next week I came around on Wednesday morning to see if he and a couple of the guys wanted to help fill orders in the warehouse. He said he couldn't that day, and then asked if I ever got up to North Memphis Liquors on Thomas Street.

"Yeah, I'm up there at least once a week, why?"

"Can you take a note to my girlfriend? She be around the parking lot up there sometimes."

"Yeah, sure."

"Gimme something to write on." I tore a piece off an envelope, gave him a pencil, and he sat there for a minute. He handed me this note.

Over the next few weeks, I asked about Velma every time I went there. Nobody ever knew where she was. I never saw James again, but I've kept the note for fifty years. If anyone knows Velma, tell her James loves her and needs her phone number.

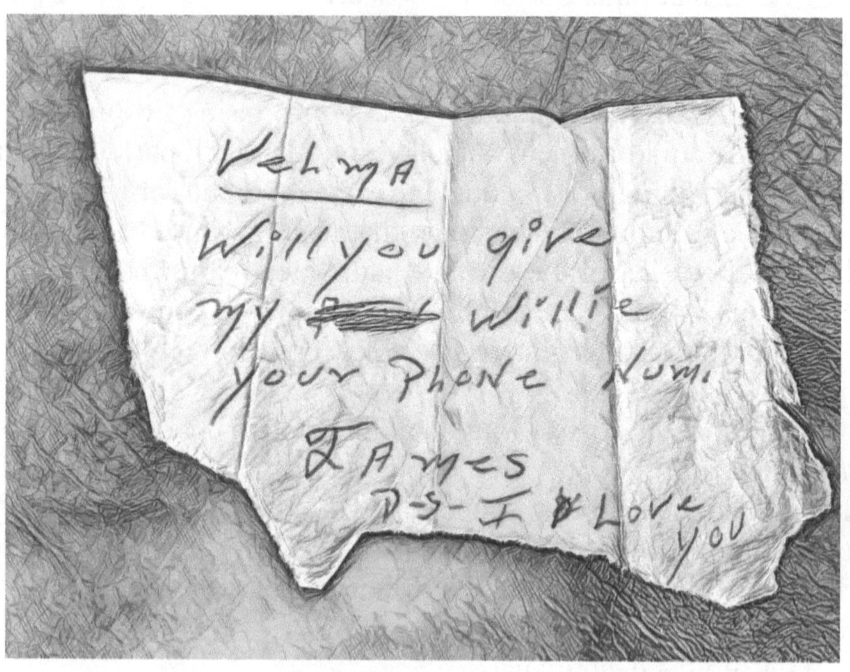

The Danish Table

How I remember Peggy.

One of my favorite stops on the liquor truck route was this little restaurant and bar by what is known as the "old bridge" in Memphis. This is the Memphis-Arkansas bridge which was built in the early 1950s, and is directly south of the Harahan and Frisco railroad bridges. The "new bridge," aka the Hernando Desoto bridge, was built in 1972, hence the colloquial name.

The neighborhood around the old bridge always fascinated me. It was known as the French Fort neighborhood, because Fort Assumption, built by the French, had been built there in 1739. Before that, it was the site of a huge Chickasaw village and still sported several ceremonial mounds overlooking the river. The Marine Hospital, kind of an old folks home for men who had worked their lives on the rivers and inland waterways of the U.S., was about the only thing still in operation when I was delivering liquor, except two motels, a Holiday Inn and a Quality Inn. Attached to the Quality Inn was a restaurant and bar curiously named the Danish Table. I ate there a few times but never got a Scandinavian vibe from the place at all. They seemed to serve what every other restaurant in Memphis served: smothered steak, fried fish, porkchops, boiled vegetables, cakes and pies. This was 1972, long before barbecue became a thing in Memphis.

The first time I delivered to the place, I rolled three cases in and asked the guy behind the bar where I was to put the liquor. He said something like, "Let me get Peggy," and went in the room behind the bar. Peggy appeared, as if out of a 1962 Mickey Spillane pulp novel, hair teased and lacquered by what looked to be a full can of Aquanet. Her remarkably curvaceous body was squeezed into a low-cut cocktail dress (it was 10 o'clock in the morning). She posed with her hand on her hip, and staring into my eyes like she could read my very soul, said, "Follow me, sugar."

She must've been about forty. I followed her into a small closet where they kept the liquor. I turned around and handed her the invoice, and after what seemed to be an eternity looking her over, I managed to say, "I'll call out what we brought and you check it off, just to make sure it's all here." She stared at me with a bemused expression. She clearly knew she had me ruffled.

"Two quarts of Jack Daniels."

"Check." She pretended to put a pencil to her tongue and made a huge deal out of checking the item off her list.

"One fifth of vermouth."

"Check."

"One fifth of Grenadine."

"Check."

"Six quarts of Gilbeys Gin."

"Check."

I moved the top box off the two-wheeler and opened the next box. I was bent over, slightly, and when I looked up, she was bent over, facing me. The closet was no more than five or six feet long and maybe four feet wide, so we were standing very close together. There, at eye level, two feet from me, was the most perfect cleavage I had experienced in my short life. The laws of gravity and brassiere engineering were being seriously tested, and my knees turned to jelly. Just at that moment, I saw what looked to be a good-sized diamond, which appeared to be somehow stuck in the inside swell of her right bosom. I froze, and then, as if some alien had overtaken my being, blurted, "What is that???"

Peggy smiled slightly, and looked further into my bewildered soul, "It's a diamond. Haven't you ever seen a diamond before?"

I blurted again, "Have you got anything else?" She didn't flinch.

"I have a ruby in my navel, but that's seen by appointment only."

I'm not sure if I fainted away for a split second. I don't remember the rest of our brief time together, or for that matter, anything that happened the rest of the day, but you can bet I tried to make the delivery to the Danish Table every week. There's something about great atmosphere and customer service that just keeps you coming back.

Free Meals Tomorrow

How I remember the Hare Krishna girl.

The first time I saw her I was instantly smitten, but, at the same time, confused. She, this willowy human with long, curly, flowing brown hair, not a smidge of makeup on her flawless face, was dancing, no, spinning, gracefully, her bare feet gliding on the pavement to the beat of the tambourine she held above her head as she chanted along with the others, "Hare Krishna, Hare Krishna, Krishna, Krishna, Hare Hare." Only two male members, drummers slapping some odd-looking instruments, sat cross-legged as the others spun 'round and 'round in a hypnotic never-before-seen spectacle right there at lunchtime on Main Street in Memphis. The year was 1972. Mr. Cox lowered his sandwich slowly and said to no one in particular, "What in the good Lord's name is that racket?"

We were sitting in the parked liquor delivery truck in the alley next to the 100 North Main building, eating the porkchop sandwiches his wife had made us that morning when we stopped by his home in South Memphis. She had packed two bottles of Barq's root beer in the grocery bag and some sugar cookies, along with the sandwiches. Mr. Cox had just remarked, again to no one in particular, that the root beer was a "fine soft drink" when the chanters began. He was an elder in a Missionary Baptist Church, and didn't allow any cussing or off-color language when he was with me in the truck. I think he liked me, because when the opportunity for a day out of the warehouse came up, he always pointed to me and told the manager, although somewhat reluctantly, he'd ride along. He had driven for years and knew where all 210 liquor stores were located in Memphis. I was still learning. We always drove by his house on Wellington Street, where, on my first visit, he proudly showed me his five Sunday suits. He had it all worked out, the blue one on the first Sunday, brown on the second Sunday, gray on the third Sunday, and black on the fourth Sunday. When I asked about the fifth suit, he proudly informed me that some months had a fifth Sunday, and he wore the blue and gray pinstriped suit on that day. He also showed me what he called his wife's "wig hats." She had fourteen of them.

The chanters had begun quietly, but were now frolicking wildly in their joyous endeavor. The drums and tambourines set a pleasing beat, and lunchtime strollers stopped to take in what surely had never before been witnessed on a Memphis thoroughfare.

"I think they're some kind of monks or something," I said to Mr. Cox's question.

"Look like some monk-ees to me," he chuckled. "That bunch looks like some of yo peoples. They hippies?"

"I don't know. I've never seen people dressed like that in real life. Wanna go over there and take a look?"

"No, sir, I wouldn't touch them folks with a ten-foot pole," he said, straining to see what was going on.

"Well, I'm gonna go. They'll probably be in jail as soon as the cops see them."

"And I'll be settin' right here, thank you. That ain't none of my business," he said as he returned to the pork chop sandwich.

A small crowd had gathered, several men in suits, curious shoppers, and porters from the cotton classing rooms on Front Street, all glancing at one another and back to the roiling group of white and saffron-robed dancers.

"Hare Krishna, Hare Krishna, Krishna, Krishna, Hare Hare. Hare Rama, Hare Rama, Rama, Rama, Hare Hare," they sang in ragged unison, spinning and spinning in a seeming state of ecstasy. The men all had the typical markings down their foreheads and nose. I know now that it's called a tilaka, and made with sacred clay, but back then it just looked like bird shit to me. They were the weirdest looking bunch I had ever seen, up-close. The girl twirled and flowed like some alluring apparition. I was transfixed.

It suddenly occurred to me that I had never truly found my people. Growing up in the Delta I had reluctantly played football, hunted deer when I had no interest in killing anything, hung out with some unpredictable psychopaths-in-training, and tried halfheartedly to fit in with people I had very little interest in. I couldn't wait to make my escape. Memphis was better, but still not what I envisioned as an enlightened epicenter from which to make my stand. This twirling earth mother seemed to fit the exact bill of what I was looking for. Although I tried not to stare, I couldn't keep my eyes off this fair-haired beauty.

When I got back to the truck, Mr. Cox feigned disinterest. He acted like he was reading something out of his Sunday School lesson, flipping through the pages with purpose. I let him stew for a few minutes until I could see he was about to burst. Finally, he said, "Well, I thought you had done got arrested or something, you sure stayed over there for long enough. We got to make it on down to Jerry Fanion's before his parking lot get too full-up and he have to escort us in with a shotgun."

"We've got plenty of time, they don't get rockin' till after 3 and they get their checks cashed."

He sat there for a minute as I backed the truck up and started to pull onto Main Street. "Well?"

"Well, what?"

"What was them folks doing?"

"They were twirling and singing something in a different language, some kind of foreign language."

"And whoopin' them drums, too," he said dismissively.

"Yeah, a couple of them were playing drums. There was this girl..."

He interrupted, loudly, and pointed his long index finger my way, "Ha! I knew it had something to do with that woman! I knew, as sure as you sittin' there, you wanted to get a better look at that woman. You better leave that mess alone. That ain't none of yo business. She's a Jezebel."

"A what?"

He stared at me, "You know good and well what I'm talking about. You been to church."

I'll admit, I was a little defensive, "I didn't even talk to her."

He turned away and looked out the window the whole way down to South Memphis. I thought about the twirling Hare Krishna girl.

For the next few days I tried to get a run to downtown Memphis in the hope of seeing the flock of strange birds again. Cecil, the assistant warehouse manager, asked me why I was so hot to go downtown. Every driver knew the downtown liquor stores were hard to service and to be avoided. There was always the problem of finding a parking place near the front door, or the risk of getting a ticket for blocking the street, or bums trying to steal from the back of the truck while you were unloading boxes. Memphis has always been a tough town, but in 1972, it was about as dangerous as

Newark, New Jersey. Many of the liquor stores had off-duty policemen as still-watches, sitting behind one-way glass with a 12-gauge shotgun at the ready for whatever fool might consider knocking the place over. These guys wouldn't hesitate to blow somebody out the front door. Back then they called it legal murder.

When I backed into the loading dock from my morning run, Cecil came over and whispered, " I got you set up. Got fourteen cases going to W&W on Vance, some odds and ends for Horseshoe on Beale, then up to Mr. Gaia's and back around to Cotton Boll on Front Street. The rest of the run is in North Memphis. That work for you?" he winked. "What you up to?"

"Oh, nothing, I just like to go downtown."

"That old man still got that parrot at Cotton Boll?"

"Yeah, that thing's bout baldheaded as Mr. Cox."

"Ain't he a hundred and something?'

"That's what the fella claims."

"Well, kiss my ass and call me Shorty." That was Cecil's standard comeback for every occasion. "Be careful."

The stores on Beale were easy in and out. Cheap wine and half-pints of bourbon were about all they ever ordered. The street was all but abandoned. Schwab's dry goods and a couple of pawnshops still hung on to what little business there was in the neighborhood. I had pawned my typewriter, a heavy Adler, at Nathan Novick's Pawnshop a couple of times for $15. I could redeem it for $18 within two weeks. It was as close to a banking relationship as I had come during my first year in Memphis.

I hurried through the Beale stores and made my way to Cotton Boll where I told the old man that Cecil had asked after the parrot. The man said, "Cecil used to deliver here all the time. Did he get a promotion or something?"

"Yessir, he's the assistant warehouse manager now."

"Tell him I said hey and to come down and see his old friend some time."

"Hey, do you mind if I leave the truck in your alley for a little while?"

"That'll be fine. How long you gonna be gone?"

"No more than thirty or forty minutes."

I locked the truck and beat it over to Court Square, and sure enough, as I was turning from the alley off Madison, I heard the drums and the faint sound of chanting. There they were.

They had drawn more of a crowd than the first time I'd seen them. People stood around with quizzical expressions, whispering to their friends and grinning at the sight of this strange troupe. I stood at the back of the crowd, and when I looked her way the girl gave me a knowing nod. I looked away quickly. I didn't know what to do. Surely she couldn't have remembered me. At the end of the next number, as the members began to pass the basket around the crowd for donations, the girl walked straight over to me. I froze.

"Hi, I noticed you here last week. I'm glad you came back today."

I stumbled, "Uh, yeah, I was down here, uh, I wasn't doing anything, I was just on my lunch break. Oh, I drive a liquor delivery truck. It's just a temporary thing till I get back in school. You know..." my inner voice was screaming, "Shut up!"

"So, do you know anything about Krishna Consciousness?"

"Uh, no, but I'd like to know about it."

"Good. We have a free meal every Sunday afternoon that's open to anyone. Would you come on Sunday if I invited you?" She smiled.

"Uh, yeah, I'd love to." Damn, I think I have a date!

"Okay, you're officially invited. Here's our address." She gave me a mimeographed sheet of paper with some information about the Krishna program, and a little map to where they lived, near the university.

"Promise you'll come?"

"Uh, yeah, yeah, I'll be there. I know where that is."

"Okay, see you Sunday." She bounced away toward the group. Just before she got to them she turned and smiled at me.

The drums started up, she started spinning, and I walked back to the truck. I sat there for a few minutes looking at the address on the paper: 3207 Spottswood Ave.

Bill Robison and me, Memphis, TN,
August 14, 1973. My 23rd birthday.

We had a deal with Mac. In fact, Mrs. Mac (we never knew her name) brokered the deal after we had eaten there every night for the first few weeks after we moved into the Dawnwood Cove house. It was a greasy spoon, meat 'n three cafe in the curve of Airways Blvd. just south of the old Memphis Defense Depot. One night as we were paying our tabs she said something like, "I guess y'all are going to be coming here about every night. Why don't we make it easy on everybody? With tax, your meals is $2.65. That includes sweet tea. If y'all will each give us $16.00 a week, you can eat all seven nights. It'll be like getting one meal a week for free."

Mac piped up from the kitchen, "That ain't a bad deal, anybody can see that. Helps us out, too."

So, that began our year-long seat at the table at Mac's Cafe. I figured out pretty quickly that Mac didn't like to have any leftovers at the end of the day. Mrs. Mac would come by to take our orders and cajole me into eating boiled cabbage, sweet potatoes, squash, spinach, collard greens, and other things I never knew I liked. That woman expanded my world and tricked my palate onto greatness.

Plate lunch, some meat-and-three place in Leland, Mississippi, 2014

The night after I received the invitation from the Hare Krishna girl, I somewhat offhandedly mentioned to the table in Mac's that I was going to be visiting the group for a meal on Sunday afternoon. Well, I might as well have said I was meeting the Manson family for midnight mass at their place. The comments from my seven roommates went something like this:

"Have you lost your fucking mind?"

"Hare Krishnas? They'll have you tied up and in the back of a van headed to California."

"There's no way you're going to that house. You don't know anything about those people. This sounds really dangerous to me."

"I can just see you with a shaved head, a bathrobe, and that bird shit down your nose."

"I'm gonna call your mama."

"Wait a minute, is there a girl involved in this?"

The conversation was nonstop for the next few days. I knew they must have been talking about this when I wasn't around because someone would ask me to take a walk around the neighborhood with them (which had never happened), and begin telling me some horror story about someone one of their friends knew who had a bad experience with the Krishnas or some other religious group. It was an all-out assault on what I was thinking might be my future.

When Sunday rolled around, one by one, my roommates all disappeared by noon. Carl had sworn he'd be back in time to give me a ride, but he was a no-show. I started to take the bus or hitch hike, but something told me there might be some truth in what my friends were telling me. I sat on the porch and weighed the situation. What would the deacons at the Rolling Fork First Baptist Church think if they heard I had taken up with the Hare Krishnas? What would my Mama say?

I sat on the porch alone till late in the afternoon. As my roommates trickled in at the end of the day, I received hugs and bro handshakes, I could see they were all a little embarrassed, but not a word was said about the Krishnas. Finally, someone said, "Y'all want to go to Mac's?" Everyone looked at me. "Nah, I don't want to go anywhere. I don't feel up to it tonight," I said. So, Carl lit a fire in the grill and we had hotdogs for supper.

Hippies in the wild. 1972

War and Protest

Greyhound Bus station photo booth, 1973

Willy Bearden

DATE: 25 February 1957
OCCASION: John Coleman's Writing Class
Faulkner: *It's—it's insight, the desire to see why man does what he does.*

John Coleman: What do you mean, Mr. Faulkner, in your story, "All the Dead Pilots," and I believe a story called "Honor," in which you give the impression that those people who fought in the war, after those experiences of war, will be dead the rest of their lives?

William Faulkner: *Well, in a—in a way they were. That the—the ones that—that even continued to live very long were the exceptions, and the one among them that coped with the—the change of time or—you can count them on your thumbs almost. Rickenbacker's one, but there are not too many others. Bishop, he finally drank himself to death, died last year, and the others, Victor Yeats didn't live ten years. But then in a way they—they—they were dead, they had exhausted themselves psychically, whatever it was, but anyway, they were unfitted for the world that they found afterwards. Not that they rejected, they simply were unfitted. They had worn themselves out.*

Used with permission, Faulkner at Virginia archive,
©copyright Rector and Visitors of the University of Virginia.

The day we were to march in the Vietnam war protest we got up early, had a good breakfast, bought several packs of cigarettes, and even though it was in July, found our heavy coats, (because we knew that the cops would initially throw you in the drunk tank and turn the air conditioning down real low to make you miserable), and met Stuart Brannock for lunch. He was the king of the Vietnam protesters in Memphis. Not that they had done that much, but he was in charge and knew the ropes. He was a very serious guy and I could tell that he was scared. That made me scared, but I kept thinking of the four boys from Rolling Fork I knew and went to school with; they were not in attendance. Not only were they not eating lunch with us, they were not scared at that moment, they weren't buying cigarettes, they were not doing

181

anything. They were dead, never to comb gray hair, and nothing anyone could say or explain to me was going to change that. Not the reality of their graves in the Mound Cemetery, nor their grieving parents, nor the silence from the pulpits of the Baptist, Methodist, Church of Christ, and Episcopalian churches after they were killed, nor the fact that none of them would ever had reached the age of twenty three like I was now. I remembered the pitiful sight of that Armstrong girl driving around Rolling Fork in Bucky's '65 Buick Skylark, looking small behind the steering wheel, and the baby who would never know his father. I look back today, at 73, and find that I am more anti-war than I was in my twenties. None of this has worked out for our country. We keep losing these insane wars and leaving people behind to spend the rest of their days acting out these self-conscious and ridiculous roles of heroes or patriots when all they have to show for it are bumper stickers or a baseball caps or vests with pins and patches, all the while living the hell that doesn't go away. The Vietnam vets I've known for over forty years now can't believe that the Republic of Vietnam is one of our most important trading partners. Nothing accomplished there. Ruined lives and created more untenable fantasies and untruths piled upon their already fragile psyches. I don't know if it's still like this but we tend to forget that during the Korean and Vietnam-era wars if a young man got in trouble with the law, often his punishment would include an option to go into the Army instead of going to jail. I say this to state that going into the military was many times the last workable option these usually poor young people had.

We went to Main Street in downtown Memphis to counter-protest a pro-Vietnam War rally put on by the American Legion. There were hundreds of them and about twenty of us. We had signs and chanted the popular slogans of the day. I was scared, but I marched anyway. I kept thinking about those four boys from Rolling Fork.

We didn't get arrested, and the American Legion guys mostly laughed and pointed at us or gave us the finger. I don't think we moved the needle on the anti-war sentiment in Memphis that day, but it made me feel like more of an American to give my opinion out there in the public. It wouldn't be long before even the hawks turned against the war. By the time Nixon finally brought all the troops home, 58,220 had died, 636 from Mississippi.

My stepbrother Eugene was a good kid, a sweet kid. He was adopted by my stepfather and his first wife, and was raised from the age of six by my mother. He loved her dearly. She was tough on him, making him live up to his responsibilities and commitments, which he hated her for at the time but later thanked her for saving him from a life of crime and selfishness. He had dropped out of high school in the eleventh grade, but she made him go back and finish when he was nineteen, and a couple of years older than the other kids. He was so proud of that diploma. I knew it was embarrassing for him, but just like years before when she made me learn to read, she inspired him not to settle for mediocrity.

He got married soon after getting out of high school and joined the Army, and it looked as if he had made all the right moves. Two children and a couple of promotions later, it appeared he was on his way to a great career. Desert Storm happened in there and he served with distinction. The homecoming party we had for him was inspiring.

Eugene got lost in Iraq during his last deployment in 2005. It was his third time in Iraq. He didn't get physically lost, but when he came back to his family in Georgia, he was not the same person. He had been a deacon in the local Baptist Church, a Boy Scout leader, and a basketball coach for his son's team. When he came back, he was secretive and negative, and we suspected he was smoking crack or meth or something. The only time I talked with him on the phone was a few days after he returned, and all he could talk about was how fucked up the Army was, and how fucked up the Iraq war had been, how our soldiers and the Iraqis were stealing millions in supplies every day, and the young kid soldiers were smoking meth and killing Iraqis like they were playing a video game. I was stunned. What had happened? How could he put up with that kind of criminal behavior from his own men? I could hear it in his voice, he was done for. I don't know how much truth there was in what he was telling me. I hope it was all a fabrication of his madness. I don't want to think our soldiers, our warriors, would do these kinds of things.

There was no victory celebration, no inspiring stories to tell, no sense of pride in what we were doing halfway around the world. It was Vietnam all over again, and I hated myself for ever getting sucked into this lie, this criminal act. The official stance is: "Look at us, we're building it back." I say, "Yes, but goddamnit we tore it up and killed tens of thousands of people in the process." It's the endless economic cycle that we've played since WWII. The economy gets bad, usually from some criminal mischief started on Wall Street, and we have to go somewhere in the world and tear some place up, and then play the good guys and build it all back. It's a silly way to run an economy. It's a selfish and criminal way to treat the poor people on both sides of the conflict.

After that, I didn't hear from him for a couple of years, and then when mama died, I made it my mission to find him and at least let him know that this woman who had raised him had died. Probably as much to keep myself occupied as to really find him, I searched the internet for his name. He had left the Army under a cloud, and the only thing I could find was a six-month old post on an expat bulletin board in Kuwait that he was looking to rent an apartment. I finally found one of his kids via MySpace, and Johnny told me he hadn't had any contact with his dad for over a year. He was very cagey in his subsequent messages, and I knew I wasn't getting the whole story. I finally found a work number for his ex-wife, who had moved back to Virginia after the divorce. She sounded reluctant to talk with me, but said how sorry she was when I told of my mom's death. She said their daughter might have a way to contact Eugene, and would let me know something. Sure enough, the next day I got an email from him. He was working as a security guard in Kuwait, and said he was sorry, but there was no way he could get back to the States for the funeral. He then launched into a long email tirade against his ex-wife, calling her some awful names, and how she stole everything from him. The problem was that these kids had gotten married when he was nineteen and she was seventeen. I had never seen two more devoted and in love people during their twenty plus years of marriage. I guess I'll never know the whole story, but the writer in me wants to finish the story, wants desperately for a dashing character to find Eugene and bring him back and get him some help.

But it doesn't end there. Over the past few years I've gotten strange emails from women who claim to be his fiance, or men who claim to be his friend, all usually saying that they have had news that he has been killed in Afghanistan, or has disappeared after working on a ship in the Indian Ocean, or married to an Egyptian Coptic woman. My gut feeling is that he is the one writing these disturbing emails. I have several email addresses for him, and I got so angry after the one about his being killed in Afghanistan, that I emailed him and threatened to beat his ass if I got any more communications like that. This is one of the most bizarre and heartbreaking stories I can imagine, and it's all true. I blame the Army for his troubles. They take these malleable people and imbue them with bravado and a sense of simplistic yet universal righteousness, and when they're finished with them, when they're all used up, they're left to fend for themselves, and it's rarely a good outcome. I would say to any young person who is looking for a secure profession for the next forty or so years, to look into psychology, especially post-traumatic stress disorder, or physical rehabilitation, or services for homeless veterans. This will be a booming business for decades to come.

About three years ago the messages began again. This time they were from a woman in California who wrote to me that she was a volunteer caretaker at a military hospital in Vacaville. It seemed that Eugene had been homeless for some time, although he still had a car, but was dying of lung cancer in the hospital. She sent along some photos of him in a hospital bed, looking like he weighed about a hundred pounds. He looked so lost and hopeless. It still haunts me. I went to his Facebook page and was assaulted by the huge amount of rightwing conspiracy theory memes and graphics. He apparently was a member of the 3 Percenters, a far-right "patriot" group founded around the time Barack Obama was elected president. The group's name derives from the erroneous claim that "...the active forces in the field against the King's tyranny never amounted to more than 3% of the colonists..." during the American Revolution. His posts were rambling, and disturbing, but seemed to have many followers who call him a "great patriot."

There were a couple of selfies taken in a parking lot in California, a photo of his car that simply said, "Home," and a picture of him looking across to the Golden Gate Bridge. I can't imagine how much he tried to convince himself that he was right. He truly was a man without a country at the end of his life. He died on November 9, 2016. His ashes were scattered in the Atlantic Ocean off Morehead City, N.C., in April 2017.

Eugene at the end of America.

Build Your Own Elvis

On the Wall at Graceland.

Does everything that happens to me have a precedent? It appears that every story I tell has a corollary from somewhere in my past, a story that informs my thinking, my decision-making, and my reaction, almost without having to think beyond the obvious, the thing in front of me. But how valid is that reaction? How viable, reasonable and bona fide are my rejoinders? Have I second-guessed myself into these automatic responses? Do I even hear what people say anymore? Have I formed these opinions so far in my past that I am nothing more than a walking, breathing reaction? This has me worried. Carl Jung posited that a person becomes individuated at approximately age forty, and thus slips the bonds of parental influence and becomes a singular individual, built and powered by nothing but his or her own life experiences. My question is, at what point does a person become so individuated that they no longer have the need for the possibility of dissenting opinions, revelations, wake-up calls or rude awakenings? I wonder if I could somehow clean out these automatic responses and become fresh in my approach to life and love. Maybe I should aspire to do the opposite of what I think.

I've always been suspect of people who make friends too easily. It's as if they ascribe to and endow the new friend with qualities and powers which are completely fabricated from their own selfish or delusional needs. Then, usually after a month or so, when the person does not measure up to this level of esteem or worship, the friendship crashes under the weight of reality, and the person moves onto someone else. I've often thought that rabid Elvis fans are like that, except that Elvis never disappoints because he is dead. Or different sects of Christianity. Tailor your savior to the beliefs you have cobbled together. In the case of Elvis, if you want him to be the rebel, the teenaged nonconformist, the side-burned iconoclast, that's easily done. If, on the other hand, you want the humble Elvis of the TV interviews, look no further than to his service in the Army. If you need the philanthropist Elvis, stories abound of him giving cars to poor women he would see walking by Graceland in the early mornings. Tough Elvis? See any of the dozens of movies he made. He was always the hero, kissing all the girls and beating up the bad guys. It's really the same with most religions. Make it what you want. It's a buffet out there, folks. Have fun designing your own. Need your God to be a vengeful, no nonsense God? Need Jesus to be the prince of peace? Need the Bible to back you up in your racist, sexist, or chauvinistic beliefs? Done.

I wish God would appear on TV, maybe right before the Super Bowl, and straighten us out once and for all. I wish he would lay down the rules like Coach Cain did in class that day in 1962. Honest as the day is long. Simple. Direct. To the point. No more wars. No more selfishness. No more gangs. No more killing. No more racism. No more cheating or taking advantage. I still hold to what the hippies of my youth believed in. This is my liberal credo. Be nice or leave. My conservative friends would call me naive, or delusional, but I truly believe we can be better.

Last Days in Memphis

When I left Memphis in the summer of 1978, it was for good, or so I thought. I had gotten into this dangerously lazy lifestyle where my only motivation was to work as little as possible to stay alive. One of my great ambitions back then was to cultivate a girlfriend at three or four nearby restaurants so I wouldn't have to buy groceries anymore. I could live off leftover pizza, sub sandwiches sneaked out the backdoor, fried chicken and biscuits that had been sitting under the heat lamp for a few hours, and soggy fish filets from Arthur Treacher's. I really thought about that a lot during the spring of '78.

I was living in a little 360 square foot guest house (the green shack which rented for $95 a month) close to the university. I didn't have, or want, a car. I worked as a substitute teacher two days a week on average, might paint the trim on a house every now and again, or mow a yard or two around the neighborhood. I even picked up dog turds once for the little old lady next door, and took her to Arthur Murray's Studio for her dance lesson a couple of times. I had to draw the line at the dog turds though, even though she had sort of conned me into it the first time by asking me to "get what the dog left," and being a little slow on the uptake that day, I didn't fully realize what she meant till she handed me the gloves and the paper grocery sack. Thank goodness this was wintertime and the turds were hard.

Even with that, I had a lot going for me. I had grown enough weed the summer before to keep me comfortably high for a year or more, knew where all the 25 cent beer nights were in the string of beer joints up and down Highland Street, had made a friend who ran the laundromat down the street and would let me wash and dry my clothes for free. I was living the hippie dream. And if I could've only cultivated those waitress girlfriends, I might've been able to whittle my work days down to less than ten a month. A man could dream.

A lot of this was the result of the court jester syndrome that I'd become so adept at since moving back to Memphis in 1976. I had learned to be the ultimate people pleaser, and I had perfected my jive in a succession of jobs and friendships so that at one point, at the height of my powers, I seemed to be everyone's best friend, confidante to the masses, drinking buddy extraordinaire. I was invited to parties three or four nights a week and invited to dinner almost more than I could accept, so that generally covered dinner and drinks. But the girlfriend thing was developing very slowly after a promising beginning. I'd been charming this waitress at the Pizza Inn for several weeks when she slipped me a bill for a small salad one day. I had eaten a medium pepperoni, extra cheese, salad and a Coke. Well, you know the drill. After that, I could count on the "deep discount" every time I went in there. She was never technically my girlfriend, but she came to a couple of parties with me that winter and would show up at the green shack from time to time. The rest of my prospective conquests weren't having any of it. The Black girl at Jack Pirtle's Chicken clocked my game early on and greeted me with the side-eye every time I walked up to the take out window. Same with the college student who worked at the Super Sub Sandwich Shop. The Universe seemed to be sending me some pretty clear messages that my game plan was flawed. In fact, I knew deep-down that I was coming to the end of something, I just didn't know what.

In front of the Green Shack, 1978

I've kind of alluded to the circumstances of my leaving Memphis and moving to Denver. Mine was a fairly embarrassing exit from the city. I feel like I wasn't altogether honest with my friends, certainly took advantage of some old girlfriends and left some people holding the bag, in particular my landlord who I left owing two months back rent. Also, this guy gave me a car, a '67 Mustang with a piston problem that I kept for a few months and sold for $350 so I could go on a trip to Washington D.C. with my girlfriend. I still feel bad about that. This behavior shamed me.

When I left, I didn't immediately go to Denver. I first went to North Carolina to put some money together so I could live while I was making my way in the west. I laid around my mother's house for a week or so when my stepdad came home and announced that he had found me a good job at the mobile home manufacturing plant in town. I went the next day for training, and eight hours later I was the new electrician. I lived in fear for the next few years that I might have been the cause of someone's death from an electrical fire in a mobile home in eastern North Carolina. I lasted at the factory about three weeks before I quit abruptly one night when, being four units behind the assembly line and frantically trying to catch up, the shift supervisor stuck his head in the door of the mobile home and said, "Are you just stupid, or do you not understand that we've got to get these goddamn trailers finished and out of here?" I unbuckled my tool belt and let it drop to the floor. I looked at him, wondering if I was going to cry or punch him in the face. "Look man, I'm the opposite of stupid. I'm trying my goddamn best to do this work safely and correctly, but this company isn't interested in anything but pushing these piece-of-shit excuses for houses out the goddamn door. I quit."

"Okay Professor, just quit." He turned to leave, then stopped. "And thanks for leaving me high and dry. I knew you weren't right for this job, but I felt sorry for you. Mr. Know-It-All who's got all the answers but no money, who's broke as the ten commandments and got no future. I guess that didn't mean shit to you. Guys like you... oh, fuck it."

I walked through the parking lot to my car, or rather my mother's car, and wondered how I was going to explain this away. As mad as I was, I couldn't get the sting of what he said out of my mind. Professor. Was that what they called me? Professor? I quickly tried to recount the times in the break room I had talked about my music career, the books I had read, the plans I had, and this was how they saw me? Professor? I wanted to run away from that place, from my parent's house, my bullshit life, and never see any of those people again. I was humiliated, because I knew it was true.

Colorado, 1978

The site of my epiphany. A pup tent in the
Roosevelt National Forest, Colorado, 1978.

I drove due west out of Loveland heading to a nebulous place drawn in pencil on a piece of lined notebook paper, my old Ford pickup bouncing along the gravel road at fifteen miles an hour. I thought I must surely have passed the place long ago, even got a little frightened at the expanse of wilderness, but I kept driving. I had lost track of time, and a calmness crept over me. I knew I was going to be alone for some time and I was finally, maybe for the first time in my life, free from having to perform.

I came to the wide place on the winding road that my buddy had indicated on the map. I parked, put on my backpack and began walking along the little creek. I hadn't walked more than fifteen minutes or so when I saw the rock. It was forty feet or more tall, and had big cracks running all along its sides. There was a little flat place alongside the creek surrounded by a few small pine trees that would work well for a campsite. Round stones indicated a fire ring, and even some stacked firewood nearby. I pitched my canvas Boy Scout pup tent and laid my sleeping bag out. Suddenly I felt I had made a huge mistake coming here. I was miles from the nearest person, and I hadn't considered the wild animals that might be around. Genuinely frightened, I started to pack up and hike back to the truck, but something told me to stay. The stillness held me in place, and what I had taken for fear was something else altogether. I sat for a long time, listening to the wind high in the pines and the water rushing by, till it began to get dark. I crawled into the tent and slept maybe the best sleep of my life and woke the next morning full of energy and purpose. For the next three days I went about my simple life in my little camp, cooking my meals on the campfire, washing my pots and pans in the stream, and thinking with a clarity I had never experienced about my future.

After a while I realized I had not spoken a word for days. At no time in my life had I been quiet, and I had now been humbled by simple silence. There was no need to speak. I was stunned to my core. I tried to reconstruct how this could have happened to me.

Just three afternoons before, I was visiting a friend, and he and I had sat in the waning afternoon light with mountains silhouetted sharply in the distance. We hadn't said much and there was a palpable distance created by a bad experience from several years before. He and I had gotten cross-ways over a woman, and hadn't spoken in three years or so. As time passed I think we both knew we had been friends only in passing. Friends of convenience. But here I was, sitting in his backyard a thousand miles from Memphis, wanting to apologize or somehow set things straight between us. I was lost and needed to believe that I mattered.

I sensed that he didn't want me there, that he didn't like me, and even though his life was full and blissful now, there remained a discomfiting sting, often touched, yet unprocessed - I had taken something from him and we were destined to remain enemies. At the same time, I believed that his essential humanity dictated that he provide me with kindness in that moment. Maybe he thought that being the bigger person would abrogate the discord which had festered between us for years.

This very human moment was, in retrospect, the apotheosis of his life, the best he ever was. Staring off into the distance after a long silence he had said to me, "When was the last time you were alone, I mean truly alone? When was the last time you did not speak for an extended time, or had nothing to add to the conversation, or no one to entertain?" He leaned forward in his chair and then looked at me with concern. "You need to take a minute and step out of your frantic life, and I know the place you need to go. It's only an hour or so from here, but it will seem like a very long way. Want me to draw you a map?"

"Sure, like, where is it?"

"You'll see." He stood, smiled at me and said, "Hey, let's cook some burgers, and you can get a good night's sleep and be fresh in the morning."

By the time I walked back to the pickup I had changed. I was a different person. My past was behind me, no longer a constant presence. I was going to make it. I wasn't sure what "it" was, but I knew that I had changed. I was twenty-eight, and I was done with the old ways. My plan of getting girlfriends who worked at restaurants seemed ridiculous, as did much of my life over the past ten years. I was ready for some kind of success, and I knew the key was me and my everyday habits, my behavior and expectations. The memory of the incident at the mobile home factory still made me flush with embarrassment, but I was facing the uncomfortable truths about myself, one step, one lesson at a time. What a gift I had been given.

Returning from the mountains, I was changed. I still had fun, but I had a new edge. At my core I became all business. I didn't know a lot *about* business, but this is how I imagined businessmen acted: you got your chores done before anything else.

Suicides

An abandoned service station, Highway 61,
Coahoma County, Mississippi.

I've known a surprising number of suicides. Maybe everyone has suicides in their lives, I've never thought to ask, but I can rattle off a dozen or so without thinking too hard. Selmer Bishop blew his brains out when I was nine. He was my first suicide and the first person I ever knew who used their big toe to pull the trigger of the shotgun while the barrel was in their mouth. He had stolen a bunch of money from his wife's daddy, and the old man was out to kill him. Selmer drove his pickup to the creek bank just north of town and ended things. They said the radio was still on when they found him. I often wondered what tune serenaded him when he finally got up the nerve to do it. I would see his wife in the grocery store for years after that looking like no amount of money was worth what she had gone through. They said at the funeral she slapped the shit out of her daddy and then hugged him. She was a mess for a long time. Mama fixed her hair for years, and I think it made her uncomfortable, never knowing what to say.

The guy in Colorado who had given me the great advice about being quiet and had drawn the map to the camp spot beside the big rock and the stream was the last. Over the years we talked every year or so, but it seemed he was always chasing something that was just beyond his reach. He tried writing, being a guitar player, a mountain guide, a ski instructor, teaching, and a dozen other things, but he always ended up dejected. His marriage ended after thirty years, and he became despondent. His calls gained in frequency and worried me because he sounded so frantic. Even though he was trying to sound upbeat, I knew this would come to a bad end.

The last time I heard from him was in late November of 2010. He left a message that he was visiting his mother in Mississippi, and wanted to come by to see me. I returned his call and left a message, but I didn't hear back from him. His brother called to tell me that he had committed suicide the day before. The personal problem we had a few years before the Colorado incident made his death even more painful. It had been my fault, and I still feel bad about it. Thirty years before he had supplied me a path to becoming an adult, a place of solitude and sanity that I had never experienced before. I will always be in his debt.

The Wisdom of Lance

Lance, 1978.

In January of 1976, feeling a great need for a change of scenery, I moved from Memphis to Jackson, Mississippi to play in a band with some friends, and like most beginnings of bands, we thought this was the one. We were called The Columbus Flood Band, after this Black guy we knew in Rolling Fork, who was Muddy Waters' cousin. We lived in this huge house in a Black neighborhood in Jackson, the living room filled with guitars, drums and PA gear. The band wasn't very good, but we always seemed to have gigs at fraternity houses and bars in Hattiesburg at the University of Southern Mississippi. The money was bad, the gigs were worse, the drinking and debauchery were rampant, and the band quickly fell apart. By August, I limped back to Memphis, and found myself having to start all over again. I rented a little green shack in the backyard of a duplex near the University and began another adventure, but that's not the story I want to tell here.

In the band, we had this guy, Lance, who played lead guitar. He was skinny, unhealthy looking and generally a B+ guitarist for the first two sets, till he got the twelfth beer down, and then he slowed the tempo about five beats per minute and became a D+ guitar player. You couldn't slow down and stay with him, because he just kept getting slower and slower. I can't tell you how many times I shot him the look of death from across the stage, him standing there with his red Gibson SG and a shag haircut, a Kool filter king cigarette hanging out the side of his mouth, thinking he was playing his ass off. And he drank like that day in and day out. Schlitz tall-boys all day long.

I remember a night near the end of our band's journey when we had gotten pretty drunk at this country joint where we were playing, and going back to this crummy apartment at about 3 AM. I was so mad at him that I decided to confront him about his drinking. I didn't want to say anything about how he slowed down when he was drunk because that would have been the absolute end of our friendship, and I didn't want to say anything mean that would hang with him for years. I suggested to him that I was worried about his drinking. You know, just generally concerned about his health.

The conversation went like this:

Me: "Hey man, I gotta talk to you about something."

Him: "Yeah? What's on your feeble mind? Haha. Just kidding man."

"Yeah, hey man, I've been with you for the past two days, nonstop, and I noticed that you haven't eaten anything. Nothing. And I was just concerned that you might need to, at least, eat a little something. I'm not saying anything about your drinking, but you know as well as I do that you have to eat sometime. You can't just drink beer."

Lance just looked at me and didn't say anything for a few seconds. He looked like he was getting some tears in his eyes. He finally spoke. "Man, thanks. I don't know what the fuck's up with me these days. You're right, I do need to eat. Man, Willy, I love you man. I swear I'll start eating."

"Hey, that's cool. That's all I'm saying. Look, I'm heading down to the Qwik Stop for some chicken and jo jo potatoes, let me get you something."

"Man, I love you. Lookin' out for a brother. That's solid of you."

"OK, so what do you want?"

"Yeah, man, uh, get me a wing."

"A wing? One wing? Man that's not very much chicken. You sure you don't want anything else?"

"Naw, that's cool. Hey, and could you pick me up a six of tallboys?"

"Be glad to, man."

A wing? A fucking wing? I brought it back and he ate it. Took him about fifteen minutes, but he ate it all. I was kind of done with him after that. It wasn't that I didn't like him or anything, but I was just done.

The band stayed together for another month or so and split up, vowing to put it all back together someday, bigger and better than ever. That's a funny thing about being in a band. I've never left a band without making plans for getting back together "real soon" even though you generally never want to see those guys again. In the musician's mind it's never himself that is the cause of the band being unsuccessful, it's those other guys who show up late, preen, slow down, drink too much, do too many drugs, piss off the club owner, run off with a waitress, or any of a hundred reasons. Truth be known, a lot of musicians are a pretty fucked up bunch.

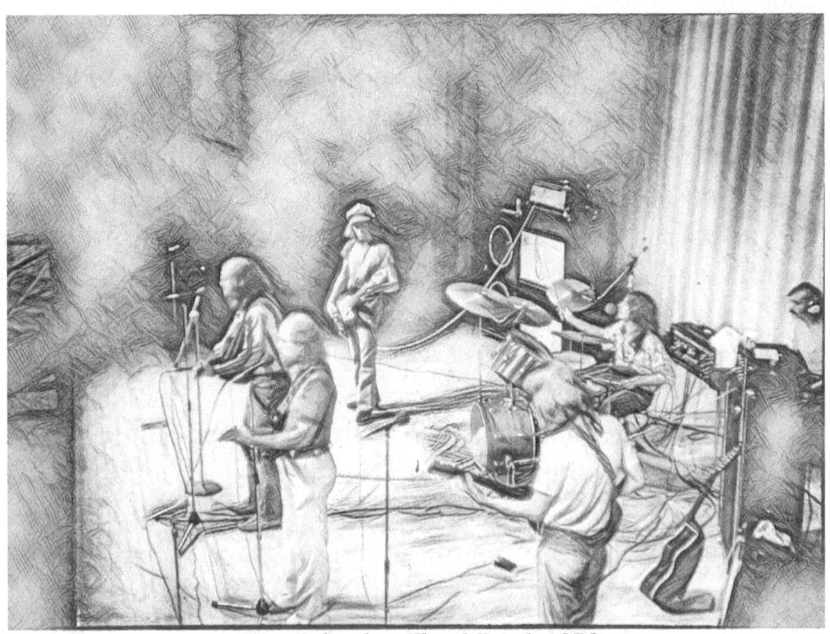

The Columbus Flood Band, 1976.

About fifteen years after that chicken wing incident, Lance called me out of the blue one day and said he had been living in Memphis for a few months, working as an optician at this eyeglasses place at the Mall of Memphis. It seemed like a most bizarre and random thing, but there he was. We made plans to get together within a couple of weeks, but I was busy at the time and didn't get back with him for about six weeks. When I did, I invited him over for a Sunday lunch and some guitar playing in the afternoon. He asked if I could pick him up, as he didn't have a car. I went over to his Parkway Village apartment in the late morning, and as we drove toward my place he asked if we could stop and get some beer. "Sure, there's a Walgreens right down the street."

"Are you gonna drink?" he asked.

"No, man, I have a really heavy day tomorrow, and I need my clarity. I don't drink that much anymore. A little wine with dinner sometimes, but that's about it."

"Cool. I was just wondering how much to buy. You know, after the band broke up, I had a fender-bender and got arrested for DUI. Then about a year later I got stopped out at the reservoir and got another one. They took my license for a year, that time. Then, I got stopped at a roadblock one night and got another one. You know, after that much shitty luck you just have to sit down and have a long talk with yourself. I decided, right then and there, that I wasn't going to drive anymore." He delivered this last line to me as we were walking into Walgreens, where he bought two six packs of tallboys - just for himself.

At lunch he ate about as much as my four-year-old daughter, and after he smoked a couple of Kools outside in the backyard, we went to my studio.

Lance and I played some of the old songs, rehashed some of the old stories except he didn't remember much, and we sat through some uncomfortable silences till I was ready to take him home. I gave him an acoustic guitar after he told me he had pawned his beloved SG when he decided to come to Memphis, and he had never redeemed the ticket. We never talked about why he had come to Memphis, though maybe he thought a fresh start would do him good. He never asked me for anything beyond a ride, so there was never any kind of ulterior motive when we got together. The few times I saw him over the next year he told of going out to clubs with work friends, and he had gone to a minor league baseball game, and even to Libertyland with a girl he knew. Our infrequent visits fell into a comfortable pattern, and I kind of looked forward to touching base with him. He was more stooped and shaggier every time I saw him, but there was something oddly pleasant about being around Lance, something that reminded me of who I had been many years ago. One afternoon, just before he moved back to Jackson, we were sitting around, and I apologized to him for being overbearing when we had the band. He said he never thought of me as overbearing, and that our band was the best one he'd ever played in. The idea that The Columbus Flood Band was the high point of his music career made me sad. We were pretty terrible, not *really* terrible, just ordinary and uninspired. His memories were quite different from mine, and I wasn't sure who was right, but maybe that's okay, too. It simply was whatever each of us needed it to be.

Several years later, Lance called to say he had met a woman online and was going to the Netherlands for a couple of weeks to visit her. I started to try to talk him out of it, but he seemed so happy that some woman had fallen for him. Lance said that she loved the songs he had written and recorded for her, and I just couldn't bring myself to warn him of the likelihood of a scam to take what little money he had. I'm sure he had sent photos of himself when he was in his twenties and looked like a rock star. Boy, would she be in for a surprise. The years, the beers, and the cigarettes had not been kind to Lance. He was stooped, wrinkled beyond his years, and his hair always looked like it hadn't been washed for a week. But he called me a few weeks later to say that he was engaged and would be moving to a small town outside Rotterdam within days. He wanted to know if I wanted any of his stuff, since he was only taking his guitars and clothes.

It seems that in his brief two weeks in the town, he had become a blues legend, playing nightly at the local tavern. The girl, Leny, had turned out to be a lovely woman who worshiped the ground Lance walked on, and was doubly pleased when he immediately became the most famous person in town. Lance told me that the beer in the Netherlands was much better than what he had been drinking for all these years in the States. Leny apparently had a house and a little money, or at least a good job, so Lance wouldn't have to work beyond playing music. Her family and friends had welcomed Lance with open arms. Life was good.

A couple of years later, in 2007, I got an email in broken English from Leny, who told me that Lance had gotten sick a few weeks before and had decided to come back to the U.S. for tests. He checked into a hospital in Jackson, Mississippi, to be near his family. Funny, I didn't know anything about Lance's family, except I remembered that his sister was married to a man from the Mississippi Band of Choctaw Indians. The doctors discovered stage four lung cancer, and Lance died in the hospital just a week later. Leny told me Lance talked about me all the time, regaling her with stories of the band, the times we had back in the seventies, and how he had reconnected with me in Memphis. She said she loved him so much, and that they had had nearly five wonderful years together. He had played at the tavern on weekend nights and was a local treasure. He made a place for himself among people he might never have known otherwise, all on the whim of an internet girlfriend. He became the star he had never been in the U.S., and it was a role that suited him perfectly. I could imagine him, pedaling around the small town on his bicycle, people waving, saying to their friends, "There's Lance, the Blues musician from America." He never gave up, never really questioned the fact that he was a rock and roll star. He lived out his dream.

Lance was the source of two of the best cautionary stories I've ever been told; the chicken wing and his decision to stop driving. I have told those stories more times than I can count, and in some small but kind of fucked up way I hope I honor the life of Lance by keeping a little of him alive. They say a person dies twice. Once, when your body stops working and you are no longer in attendance. But the second time a person dies is when the last person who knew you and your story dies. The last person to ever utter your name. Then you are truly dead. I think about this a lot. Lance.

Mr. Tarleton

Mr. Tarleton's house. From a dream.

I hadn't had a presence in Rolling Fork for many years, aside from a visit or two a year, usually while passing through to New Orleans or Jackson, but in 2000, I started playing music with some guys from the Delta. We formed a band called The

GrayHounds. For the next ten or so years we played in the Delta and over in the Ouachita Mountains of Arkansas, where three of the guys lived. We had a great time, and it reignited something in me that had been covered up for a long time. The act of playing music with a group of like-minded people is one of the most powerful feelings I have experienced. It doesn't seem like such a big thing, but something happens when everyone is deep into a groove. It's almost like you can read your bandmate's mind. You see and feel where the other person is going, all in rhythm, nuance, and dynamics. It is a unique experience.

Playing with the band and being around Rolling Fork again after so many years, I felt the need to reconnect with the Delta. It was speaking to me on so many levels. I realized that much of my new work had a lot to do with the Delta and Southern culture. It seemed I had spent a lifetime trying to get away from there, but now the call was clear and important. I needed to experience the Delta on my own terms. I bought a house along Deer Creek, just up from the school. It had been built just after the 1927 flood by Sam Rosenthal, the longtime mayor of the town. It was a good house: red brick, big yard, high ceilings, plenty of rooms, and the nicest front porch I could imagine. And although I could only spend a few days here and there, mostly working on writing projects and editing on films, it felt right. I was back in my old hometown.

On one of my trips to Rolling Fork over the first few months, I visited Mr. Tarleton, the Issaquena County sheriff for almost 40 years. I visited him out of courtesy and respect and to let him know I was in town and what my intentions were, even though I was a bit confused about that myself. He knew I had bought the house and was coming down to write and edit my films. His network was still as alive and thorough as it had been 30 years ago, but he needed to see me come to him. We both knew that. Writing it here it seems like I was going to see Don Corleone from the "Godfather" movies, and I guess it was somewhat like that. He received me with a warm handshake and told me how proud of me he was.

"I've been keeping up with you, and I'm glad you've done well," he said as we walked through the high-ceilinged house, complete with an old Southern pine roll-top desk, an ornate French bombe chest and other beautiful pieces filling every available space. The walls featured a signed Carrol Cloar print and several oils by Marie Hull, completely unlike what I would have imagined in a Southern sheriff's house. "You coming back down here to run for Governor?" he laughed. "Actually, you'd make a good mayor for Rolling Fork. You could do right by a lot of these folks who sure did right by you when you were a youngster."

I laughed. "I'm afraid I'd be the worst mayor they ever had. I don't do meetings well, and I am way past arguing with anybody about anything." He gave me a big grin.

We sat on the broad gallery of his home, a beautiful place that had been built in the 1840s, behind what is now the mainline levee. He had bought the rundown house for little of nothing at a tax sale, had it cut in half with a chainsaw and moved to this lot he had on the west bank of Lake Washington, an oxbow lake that was once a part of the Mississippi river channel. Oxbow lakes, for the uninitiated, are big loops in the old river channel that get cut off at some point by the river current creating a new channel through the narrow part of the loop. There are oxbow lakes all up and down the lower Mississippi. Moon Lake, near Clarksdale, is probably the most famous. Tennessee Williams seemed to always include a line or two about someone who had been killed or experienced some nefarious pitfall at the Moon Lake Casino in the crazy 1930s Delta.

Mr. Tarleton talked and talked about things that had happened in the county over the years. He was a great storyteller, and for someone who had never lived outside this tiny county, Mr. Tarleton was a wise man with a lot of practical experience. I knew he was someone I could trust and someone I needed to listen to.

"The problem is," he continued, leaning back in his chair, "the white racist sees old Tupac Shakur hanging out the window of a Cadillac Escalade with those spinning hubcaps, shooting at 'em with a Glock or spraying the Sunday morning crowd at the Baptist church with an Uzi, and the Black racist sees the KKK or the skinheads standing in every door: the school, the factory, the grocery store, the jail, the courthouse, everywhere, trying to run his ass back to n*****town. And they're both wrong, dead wrong. Black and white people who figured this game out 40 years ago found success. Just look around, you'll see it. You haven't been back but a minute, but if you'll look you're gonna see two distinct classes of Black folks, just like the two distinct classes of white folks. When people stop gettin' their backs up about what they perceive as a slight or disrespect, they find it a lot easier to prosper and be happy in this society. I've seen it a lot in our little part of the world. A good government job with a steady paycheck will go a long way in making a fella enjoy life a little more." He sat back and looked across the beautiful lake, saying nothing for a full minute.

"So, who do you think killed Biggie and Tupac?" He spoke with the sincerity and wonderment he would use when talking about golf or fishing. The old sheriff watched my reaction to such a random question. He was clearly taking delight in throwing me a curve ball.

"What?" he grinned, "Hell, I watch those A&E documentaries all the time. We've got the same TV shows you have up in Memphis. It ain't a bit of difference here as it is there. Just people killing one another." He paused for a long minute. "I just think about those boys' families and the kids they left behind. That doesn't change. I guess I've seen my share of killin' and death, and I'm just weary of it."

His wife brought out a pitcher of sweet tea, poured the cut glass crystal tumblers full and left without saying anything. "You know I died a few months ago, don't you?"

"I knew you had been really sick, but what happened?"

"I was in the hospital and I was hurting real bad, and I heard the doctor talking to my wife and Nancy. You know my daughter Nancy, don't you? Anyway, I heard them but they weren't in the room with me. I found out later they were down the hall about fifty or sixty feet at the nurses' station, but I heard them as clear as if they were standing right at the foot of the bed. I saw myself rise above the bed and watch as they came into the room and stood around me. They were saying things like, 'Well, he's gone to be with Jesus now,' and things like that. They were both crying. That surprised me for a second, and I realized that I had died. I thought, 'Damn, I'm dead.' I didn't hurt anymore. At that moment I calmly asked God if I could live some more. I told him that I wasn't scared to die, but I just wasn't ready. And, I went right back into my body, and buddy, it hurt like hell. I almost regretted being alive again, but I knew I'd be alright. It really happened. I haven't told too many people, but I knew you'd understand."

We sat in silence for a while as the light faded. He had been so matter-of-fact about dying that I didn't want to break the moment. I could see that he was still considering the experience, "chewin' on it" he would have said, but was clearly satisfied to have shared it with me.

Mr. Tarleton wasn't the kind of person to show any weakness or lack of confidence, so by the time he looked up at me, he was back to his old self. "I once had this old Black man who lived out by Goshen. You might remember him, they called him Uncle Wash. George Washington Jones was his given name. Well, he came into the office and complained that ole Norbert Reese had been shooting at his feet every day when he walked by Norbert's house on the way to the store. You remember Norbert, don't you? Bad dude, crazy as a shit-house rat. Now, you know and I know that Norbert wasn't trying to kill Uncle Wash, or even hit him. If he had wanted to kill him, he would have done it without battin' an eye. He was just fuckin' with him, shooting at his feet with a .22. He'd probably sit there on the porch and wait for that old man to walk by every day."

"I had a talk with Norbert right after I got elected the first time. I wasn't but 23 years old, full of piss and vinegar," he said wistfully. "I told him that I wasn't going to be comin' out to Goshen all the time to attend to him, and the best thing he could do was to straighten up and fly right."

"What did he say to that?"

"He looked at me hard, and told me he'd kill me, but I said, 'Not if I kill you first.' I had my hand on my gun, and I would have killed him right where he was standing. Norbert and I hadn't had any problems till this business with Uncle Wash came up, and I guess by that time I'd been in office for about six years."

"What did you do?"

"I thought on it for a good while, and I told Uncle Wash that if I was him I'd find a different way to walk to the store." And he winked. That was Mr. Tarleton.

"But the best Norbert Reese story happened about ten years ago. These ole boys from Jackson were hunting out in the Delta National Forest and got lost. Well, that wasn't anything new, we always were having to go out and find these boys who thought they were big-time deer hunters. It was kind of like that movie 'Deliverance,' except without the corn holin'." He laughed at his own joke, and I knew then that he had told this story many times. He was on a roll. "Seems these guys had been lost since the morning before and their buddies had gotten worried. It was November and cold as a witch's titty, and we have had some of these lost folks die out there. They don't respect the wilderness, and that's some damn big woods out there. You can walk a hell of a ways and not see sign of civilization, especially if you're walkin' in circles.

Anyway, we had about 30 people getting ready to head out and find them before it got dark. One night out there in the cold is one thing, but two nights is something else, and I knew they had probably gotten wet and eaten what food they had with them, if they had anything. We were getting ready, and up comes Norbert in that old pickup of his, pulling a horse trailer. Hell, I hadn't seen him in years, and I thought it was strange. But, you know, maybe he was hunting out there and was just stopping by to see what was going on.

He got out of the truck and came right over to me. His hair was real long and his old beard was hanging all down to his chest. He had gotten gray too. He looked like one of those old Civil War generals, Jeb Stuart or Stonewall Jackson or somebody. He said, 'Sheriff, I come to help you find those men.' And I told him that was neighborly of him. Oh, I forgot to tell you that Norbert had on an old hunting coat that looked like it was from the 1930s, and he was wearing a pair of striped pants, and I knew that those had been his daily wardrobe when he was in the penitentiary up in Parchman, years ago. Did you know that he got sent there in the mid-fifties for shooting a boy that came out to pick up his sister for a date? I think he did two years hard labor. Anyway, I told him to go wherever he thought he might find them, and he got on his horse and took off through the woods."

"Did he find them?" I could see the scene playing out before my eyes; bad guy turns good and finds the lost men in the woods. The town celebrates.

"Well....hmmm," and he held up a hand, as if to say, "more to come." Then he continued. "When we found them right before sundown that afternoon, they were wet and cold and huddled together way the hell down the river, almost to Valley Park. They must've walked 10 or 12 miles. And, boy, were they glad to see us. When we finally got back to their deer camp one of the guys thanked me again and said that earlier that morning they had heard something crashing through the brush and they thought it might be a deer or a wild hog or even a bear, but he said a man with a big ole long beard and wearing convict pants, riding on a horse, came right to them and just sat there looking at them. Well, they were near about crying, just so relieved that they had been found. He told me, 'I said something like, thank you so much for finding us, we thought we were going to die out here.' He said the man snatched the reins and the horse kind of bucked, and he looked at them with those black eyes and said, 'Hellfire fella, I've been lost in these woods for 25 years,' and dug his spurs into the horse's flanks, tore through the underbrush, and was gone."

"Damn. They must've been scared out of their minds."

"Yep, that ole boy said he sat right down and cried like a baby. He was terrorized." The sheriff paused for effect. "That Norbert is one more son-of-a-bitch."

He smiled and looked out across the lake. A minute later he turned to me and looked me straight in the eye.

"I know you boys thought I was hard on y'all back when you got out of high school, but you gotta understand that we didn't know what in the hell was going on. One minute, y'all are the Delta Valley Conference football champs, and the next minute it looks like the damn Rolling Stones have invaded. I knew y'all were smoking marijuana, but I didn't know anything about what it did to you. I thought y'all might all go crazy and start killing people or something. That mess with Charles Manson had us all in a tizzy. I know it sounds crazy now, but with the information we had back then, we were scared shitless. We had been hearing for 20 years that the communists were gonna infiltrate and bring us to our knees, and this looked like it."

"I know. We didn't know what was going on any more than you did. We just knew that things were changing, and that we were supposed to have something to do with that change. You know, the war, civil rights, women's lib, it was all up in the air. That's why I got out of here. I was scared for years to come back. I thought I'd wind up in Parchman, and that scared me to my core."

"I remember we followed y'all around, wondering if we could bust you, but I never thought of y'all as criminals. They ought to legalize that shit. I don't smoke it myself, but after a while I didn't see much harm in it for most folks. It sure cut down on the fightin' around here."

"It did, didn't it? The rednecks got mellow."

"So did the Blacks," Mr. Tarleton chuckled. "Now we got cocaine, crack, meth, all that bullshit."

"Don't forget alcohol."

"Worst of 'em all. I'm glad I'm out of the whole mess."

There was a commotion coming from the front of the house that broke our reverie; people greeting, children talking and running, doors opening and closing.

"That's my daughter and her bunch," he said, looking at me with a fake withering glower. "I love 'em dearly, but they do wear me out."

Just then, a tiny head peeked around the corner of the doorframe.

"Papaw!" this little boy yelled, and ran to Mr. Tarleton, jumping in his lap and hugging him tightly. The boy leaned back and looked at him for a second and hugged him tight again. I could see that Mr. Tarleton was moved almost to tears.

"Hey monkey, say hello to Mr. Willy," his voice catching.

"Hey, Mr. Willy," the boy dutifully said, then turned back and settled into the old man's lap.

"I'm going to push on. Looks like you're gonna have your hands full."

"Come on stay for supper. I don't know what we're having, but it's always good."

I stood and looked out at the lake, the afternoon having lost to twilight.

"I need to get back to town."

Mr. Tarleton stood up with the boy in his arms, then lowered him to the floor. "Go in and help your mama and your grandmaw."

"Yessir," the boy answered.

"And say goodbye to Mr. Willy."

"Bye bye," he looked at me and smiled, then turned toward the door.

"What else you got to say?

The little boy, he couldn't have been more than 4 years old, stopped and looked at Mr. Tarleton, and then at me, smiled a big smile and said, "See you in church on Sunday!" He looked to his grandfather for approval.

By the time I got to my car tears were streaming down my face. That one simple sentence from a 4-year-old summed up everything

I had missed in my life, everything I had longed for but never felt. Those times in elementary school when I frantically scanned the audience at the Christmas play or the little league baseball game, or any of a hundred events where a kid needs to see the proud faces of their parents. Nothing. Mr. Tarleton had clearly done right by his grandson, and if I had to bet, he had done right by everyone in his orbit. I don't remember how old I was when I stopped searching the crowds, but I did.

Pete and Repete

Pete, Jeff and me, 1954.

There is a photograph I found of me, my brother Jeff, and our friend Pete, taken on the swingset in our backyard in 1954. Jeff is two years older than me, and Pete and I have our arms draped over his shoulders. Pete is a year older and wearing coveralls in the picture, snotty nose and a big smile on his brown face. I lost contact with him after we both got out of high

219

school, but I heard he was the drum major of the Mississippi Valley State College marching band, and once marched in the Rose Parade in Pasadena. Pete was the first gay person I knew. I didn't realize that till much later. He lived with his grandmother, Alice Bailey, who was our maid and the woman who raised me from birth to early adolescence. I remember sitting in her lap, Pete on her right leg and me on her left, her fan with the picture of Jesus snapping back and forth, pushing the August afternoon heat around our little heads. In my memory, I am looking up at her smiling face. They were my safe place, and I don't even know what happened to them, Alice surely dead these many years, and Pete, what of Pete? I hope he's had a good life. Alice used to call us Pete and Repete.

As I sit in the liquor store with my friend Clark on these long Delta nights I begin to feel it creep back into me, like some slow warmth or the meaty satisfaction of being right where you know you're meant to be. Home. It has come to me that slowly, yet determinedly and in phases. I was back in Rolling Fork. I began by trying, as I have throughout my career, to be everyone's best friend. My friend Charles once told me that he was a visitor at the LBJ ranch outside Austin, the year after President Johnson left office. He was a guest there with his wife's grandparents, a well-placed couple from the Delta who had been chummy with the Johnsons for many years. Charles said that on the second day they were there, he saw the President sitting by himself on the patio in the early morning chill. He went over and sat with the great man, and the conversation went something like this (although I'm sure there is a little Delta embellishment added for good measure I would bet that it is essentially true):

"Son, what kind of business are you pursuing?"

"Mr. President, I'm in my second year of law school at Ole Miss."

"Well, I've worked with many fine lawyers in my time, but I myself was a school teacher."

"Yessir, I knew that."

"Well, if I can give you some unsolicited advice, I'll tell you this. You treat everybody you work with like they were your best friend. Do everything you can to make them feel the same way about you. Loyalty is the most important thing you can share with people you work with. But, if they won't let you be their best friend, you be their worst goddamned nightmare. Make 'em seize up every time they see you, or even think about you."

That approach (the best friend thing, not the worst nightmare) has served me well in the past and was certain to work here, or so I thought. That brought about what I can only describe as the Steinbeck Syndrome, or maybe the Cannery Row Condition. Within days of arriving back in Rolling Fork it seemed the whole town knew I was easy pickings. I had itinerant tree trimmers, yard mowers, house painters, gardeners, maids, roofers and even a "personal assistant" knock on my door, all walking, mind you, no sign of transportation or tools of any kind, yet each ready to begin work at that very moment, and for the ridiculously low price of $35 on average. Well, who wouldn't go for a deal like that? I figured I could provide a little economic stimulus and get some much needed work done around the house. But like Steinbeck's Doc in "Cannery Row," my magnanimity proved to be the perfect ingredient for mishap, misadventure, and misunderstandings.

Part of this was certainly self-inflicted. My penchant for putting myself into bizarre situations just to see how I would react had thus far proven to be a safe if not selfish endeavor, but I quickly saw that I was way beyond my area of expertise. I was operating in the rarified atmosphere of professionals whose skill sets were superior in every way to mine. This was not the arena for a dilettante such as myself. Years, decades, generations of craftiness, artful bullshit and deal-making, though usually with some fatal flaw, had rendered me helpless to the onslaught of subplots, additions, and changes in plan I suffered, usually in something as seemingly straightforward as raking the yard.

But let me add this, and be very clear about it; I have come to know and believe this - that hardpressed people will do whatever it takes to get food to eat, a place to stay, and some level of security in their lives. It's heartbreaking on one hand and absurd on the other. Absurd, I guess, if you're only looking at it and not living it every day. The 'I gotta do what I gotta do' school of behavior or existence is extant and more common than any one of us might want to believe. It is the basis of most crime, the overriding factor of all doctrine or system of belief, and the safe place to reside when nothing else will suffice. I laugh about my bizarre encounters, but right there at their core they are the manifestation of the piled-upon decades of slavery, of the inherent avarice of the sharecropping system, and the rigged nature of virtually every facet of life for the poor especially, in this country. Still, the inventiveness of these practitioners amazes me on some odd level that I can't explain.

Let me see if I can deconstruct a couple of encounters. Man in his early 30s, walking, comes up to me as I'm about to get in the car.

Him: "I see those limbs are tearing a hole in your roof. I'll get my crew over here with the bucket truck and take care of them for you."

Me: "That's OK, but thanks anyway. I have to be out of town all day. I'll get someone to look at it when I get back."

Him: "I can get right on it."

Me: "That's OK, thanks though." Simple as that, no?

Later that same day, I'm almost back to Rolling Fork from my day in Jackson, and the phone rings. It's Clark from the liquor store. "Hey, this guy just came by the store and wanted me to give him $350 for trimming some trees at your house. I told him he'd have to see you. Listen, I don't want to get into your business, but don't mess with that guy. I've heard he's bad about trying to sue somebody. His cousin is a lawyer."

Me: "What? I told that guy that I'd have somebody look at it when I got back to town. He's already done it?"

Clark: "You told him you were going to Jackson? That's why he went ahead and did it. He's gambling that you'll feel sorry for him and go ahead and pay him. I wouldn't give him $350 though, he'll probably be glad to get $100."

Me: "Wait a minute, I didn't tell him to do anything. I should have him arrested for coming onto my property with a bucket truck. I didn't sign a contract, see an insurance certificate or anything."

Clark: "Bucket truck? You sure we're talking about the same guy? He ain't got no bucket truck. Wasn't he walking?"

Me: "Sorry to pull you into this, I'll deal with it." Eight minutes after I pull into my driveway, he appears, as if out of thin air. Been watching for me. Walks up talking on his cell phone. "Yeah. y'all take the bucket truck around to the back of her house and get started. Tell her it'll be eighteen hundred...naw, tell her it'll be fourteen hundred since she's such a good customer. Alright, I'll be on out there in a little while. Y'all do it right and don't rut up her yard." To me: "Hey sir, how are you doing? I got everything worked out and your roof is as good as new. Wasn't much damage. I didn't charge you anything for the shingles I replaced, they were scuffed up. I came by to pick up my money."

Me: "What's your name? I didn't ask for you to do anything to my house and I sure didn't want you to be messing around up there where the power lines come in. You and I didn't have any deal at all. I distinctly told you that I'd have someone look at it."

Him: "But you told me that it was OK, so I did the work, and I've got to pay my crew and everything." So we go back and forth for a while, him saying he's sorry for the misunderstanding and me saying that we had no understanding at all. Him saying that I've put him in a bad situation, me saying that I don't care. Finally we agree that I'll give him a hundred and that he'll stay off my property from now on.

Two hours later, two guys knock at my backdoor: "How you doing, sir? We came by 'cause we helped Curtis trim your trees and replace those shingles this morning and now he done told us that you didn't pay him and he can't pay us and we were wondering if you could pay us."

Me: "Guys, you've got to take this up with Curtis. I never told him to do anything in my yard, he just went ahead and did it, thinking that I'd feel sorry for him and pay him something, which I did. I gave him a hundred, so maybe you should go and see if you can get some of that hundred before it's gone."

"Curtis said you didn't give him nothing. We'll go find him."

"Did he drive a bucket truck onto my yard?"

"Curtis ain't even got no drivers license. He had a little old janky-ass ladder wasn't even tall enough and he pushed me up on the roof."

So, later I hear that they found Curtis and since he was drunk (courtesy of me) they whipped his ass and took the rest of the money. Then he called the police the next day and told them he had been robbed, and all of a sudden I had the police over here asking me what I had to do with this robbery. The case went to court the next week and I was expected to testify for the defense. How this would play out was beyond me. Now, considering myself somewhat of having graduated from an apprentice to a journeyman in the ways of the shellgame, con, fake misunderstanding dance we do here in the Delta, I was intrigued to still be attached to this case. I fully expected to be served with papers and promptly sued for my part in this fiasco of a business arrangement.

Case #2

Early one morning a knock came at the front door. I should have known then as I know now, that no one with an intimate understanding of me or my house would ever come to the front door for anything. In fact, I had to brush away cobwebs when I opened the door to an old, skinny woman, but I opened the door and this woman said, "I was looking for your lady friend, and I'm so sorry to bother at you now, but she tole me to come by this morning and get my pay. I know she prolly gone, but I've been having some troubles and I really need my money if you can spare it. I know things are hard all over and everything, and I hate to ask on such a day.”

“How much did she owe you?”

“She owed me ‘roundabout fourteen dollars for some ironing I did for her...”

“Oh, that’s not a problem, let me get my wallet.”

“...and another twelve for last week, and let me see can’t I remember what else she been owed me,” she pondered.

“OK, you figure out what she owed you and I’ll get my wallet. I’m sure you won’t mind signing a receipt.”

“To sign a what? I don’t know nothin’ about that. Me and that lady just worked on a mouth-to-mouth type agreement.” I’d have to remember that one.

“OK, don’t worry about the receipt. I’ll get my wallet.”

When I came back to the door she was looking intently at the ground and holding her long index finger straight up in the air. “I had a rememberance that she owed me a little something for helping out back in July.”

“OK, how does fifty dollars sound? Will that cover it?”

She pondered for a moment, “I think that’ll ‘bout get it. If I remember anything else I’ll be on by.” Needless to say, for the next week or so she remembered slights in pay and old, unpaid debts that came to mind. The word was clearly out that I was back and ripe for the picking.

While I’m bitching about the Delta, let me say that it is all quaint and funny and endearing when you’re sitting in Memphis, telling someone of the quirks and eccentricities of the Delta, but yet another thing indeed when you’re smack in the middle of it. Fact: the only store open in Rolling Fork after 8 pm is the mini-mart, where they sell lots of beer, tobacco products, and fried chicken. I’ve had to go by there to pick up milk or laundry detergent or toothpaste, and they seem to have the toughest time making change. Not making change, but having the correct change on hand. Tonight I gave them a fifty dollar bill for about twelve dollars worth of merchandise. Here is the change I got back. Four rolls of nickels ($8), a huge wad of crumpled one dollar bills ($26), three rolls of pennies, ("But I don't need pennies.") ($1.50), fourteen quarters ($3.50), and some more nickels, and the damnedest thing about it was that no one seemed to think this was odd in any way. The time before, I was given rolls of quarters, which I later took to the bank and exchanged. I don't know what's going on, but it is frustrating to have to think on those terms. I started to ask for the manager, but decided it would be a fruitless conversation.

I told Clark my story of woe and he said, "What, they wouldn't give you your change?"

"No, they gave me my change alright, but they want to give me rolls of pennies and nickels, and I don't want that."

"Did they give you the correct change?"

"Yes, but... nevermind."

After all these encounters, I looked around and found myself more involved with people and their everyday lives, and I realized the circles in which I moved, the prime motivation was to avoid the exact things I was living every day in the Delta. The act of seeking out, and paying strangers to diagnose and advise and treat those problems have created a multiplicity of problems of their own, primarily isolation. It was a never-ending circle of cause and effect and reaction, and then demanding that an objective, but non-involved third party make sense out of the mess and set it all straight. It's nothing but the messiness of life, and the reality that we are surrounded by damaged, hurt and hard-pressed people. If I've learned anything in seventy plus years, it's that everybody is fucked up in some way. Everybody. We all have hard things we face every day, and experiences from childhood and adulthood that don't go away. We are tasked with making sense of the inexplicable, and parsing sanity when it is no more than a mirage. Some people understand this. I don't, but I hope to one day.

The Kansas Plains

I feel the need to tell this story even though there are no great lessons to impart and little but sadness in the telling. This memory has stayed with me for 40 years and I'm not sure if by saying it out loud I think it might ease my burden or at least share it with the world. It is the story of lost people. At various times in my life, I seem to have been a magnet for those who can find no place, no comfort in the world.

I woke up thinking about one day years ago in 1983 when I left Wichita. I was on a sales trip for Motion Picture Labs, and I had flown into Kansas City on a Monday, rented a car, and driven the four hours to Wichita. I wanted to get a feel for the landscape and to see the Flint Hills in winter, a forlorn and dramatic country with epic panoramic views of the plains. I made my rounds to the customers I had in Wichita and took several groups out to lunch or for after-work drinks. After all, that's most of what an account executive does. No one wants to see you before 10 am or after 3 pm. The free lunch is a bonus, and the drinks exist to cement loyalty. I did this tap dance all over the midwest and the far north for seven years, and I got good at it. It was a lonely life, but I managed to use my downtime well. I learned to be a better writer and a better reader during those hours waiting in hotel rooms, restaurants, and airports.

The morning of my departure from Wichita, I had a late breakfast, and just as I entered Denny's a light snow began to fall. The waitress who had waited on me the previous three mornings brought a cup of coffee to the table and said in a nasally voice, "I thought you'd have been long gone by now."

"No, I slept in this morning and then had a few phone calls to make. I'm gonna head on out in a few. I've got a feeling it's gonna take a while to get to Kansas City."

"You'd better get on the Turnpike before you get snowed in."

"I'll be OK. My plane doesn't leave till seven tonight."

"Alright, just be careful of the wind, it can knock you clean off the road out there on the open plains."

I stopped at the toll booth to get my ticket when I saw what looked like a woman standing on the side of the road about a hundred yards beyond the booth. As I got closer, I saw that it was a woman, an Native American woman, holding a little girl's hand. It was as odd a sight as I had ever seen. I stopped and asked where they were going.

"We're going up to Pine Ridge. Up to the reservation in South Dakota. Can you give us a ride?"

"Yeah, of course. Get in. I'm only going to Kansas City."

They got in the backseat, the woman brushing snow off the little girl's head and back. They sat in silence for a few minutes as I began to drive.

I broke the silence. "So, what's your name?"

"I'm Minnie and this is Dora."

"Where are you coming from? I'll bet you were freezing out there."

"I was down in Oklahoma, but things didn't work out, so I'm going home. We're Sioux. We're going to Pine Ridge."

She said this with no emotion, just like the first time she said it. I got the feeling she just wanted me to shut up.

"Yeah, OK." I turned around. "Hi, Dora, how old are you?" The girl didn't say anything.

"She's almost three."

We rode along in silence for several minutes. The snow began to fall harder, and the wind picked up. From the backseat I heard a hissing sound followed immediately by the sharp reek of spray paint or aerosol.

"Hey, what's that? What are you doing?" I turned around to see Minnie spraying paint from a can into what looked like a cardboard toilet paper tube. "What's going on?"

"This is my medicine," she said quietly. "I have to take it."

"You shouldn't...that stuff will give you..." I turned back around and stared at the road. For three hours, as we trudged against the falling snow, Minnie took her medicine every fifteen minutes or so, never saying a word. My head was pounding from the fumes, and I was afraid to light a cigarette around what surely would be a flammable mixture. We drove on slowly through the bleak Kansas landscape. I became almost frantic wondering what I was going to do with them. It began to snow harder as we approached Topeka. I decided that I would take them to the bus station and buy them a ticket to South Dakota. It was late afternoon when I pulled off the highway. I figured the bus station would be somewhere in the downtown area.

It didn't take long to find the Greyhound station. It was a squat, yellow brick building, straight out of the early 1950s, the neon sign like a weak blue smudge against the sky as the snow fell. I pulled into the parking lot and turned to Minnie.

"Hey, I'm going to put you and Dora on a bus to Pine Ridge. It's getting dark, and I've got to catch a plane in a couple of hours."

"I don't want to take a bus. I don't like the people on the bus. We can just wait here for a ride."

"No, you can't wait here in the snow. Get on the bus and get home. You'll probably be there by midnight or early morning. Come on, let's go in." My head was pounding, and I was torn by the realization that I would be rid of the paint fumes and my growing anger at a mother who could do this to her child and herself, but I equally feared what leaving them alone might bring.

"OK, let me take my medicine first," and she huffed another lung-full of paint vapor. I was so mad at her by this point that I considered calling the police to come take the child from her, but something told me that I should simply end my time with them. We walked into the bus station, and I had her sit down on a metal bench while I went to the desk and shared enough with the agent to make sure she couldn't cash in the ticket or sell it. He assured me he would see to it that she got on the bus and not get off until they reached the reservation.

My head was splitting, so I walked outside into the cold, leaned against a brick wall and lit a cigarette. I was cold as a son of a bitch, but I couldn't leave. I kept walking and back and forth to the door to make sure she was still sitting there. I got madder and madder thinking that she would drag this little kid around on her insane travels. I wondered what would happen to them when they got back to the reservation. By the time I finished my cigarette I was shivering uncontrollably. I walked back into the waiting room and told her that the ticket agent would get her on the next bus heading north. She looked at me blankly and looked away. I walked out into the fading light, got into the rental car and drove to the airport. I would be back in Memphis long before they got to Pine Ridge.

I have thought about Minnie and Dora often since that day. Dora would probably be thirty-four or thirty-five, and Minnie, probably dead. I wonder why I was meant to see the strange pair that day in a place I'd been on a few business trips before but would probably never be again. Could it have been I was there to save their lives that day? Or maybe it was the bleak memory of standing on the side of the highway in the cold or the rain, scared and questioning my own ridiculous ramblings that made me feel some kinship to these fellow wanderers. Of course, I never knew what happened to them, and even though I would love to have a lesson or revelation to share, there is nothing but a statement of facts. That is all. No hero's tale. No tidy ending. No feel-good moment. But every time I see snow falling, especially on a cold, late winter afternoon, I think of Minnie and Dora, and our journey through the Flint Hills of Kansas. That is my story, my burden.

The Irony

Me, Mama, and Jeff. 1962

As I told earlier, I once saw a white man leap a grocery store counter to chase and I guess kill a young civil rights worker who was in Issaquena county for the summer helping to register the hundreds of African Americans who had been intimidated, tricked, and lied to by white officials and landowners into assuming that they would never be able to cast a vote to decide their future. The white man, Mr. Fant, was a known

Klan member and what they called back then, a hot-head. Even white folks gave him a wide berth.

The county was probably 70% African American. There were no Black elected officials, only a couple of Black landowners, and a pitiful excuse for an elementary school for the many students who needed and deserved to be educated. It was a shameful place, Issaquena County, but no more or less shameful than any of the other eighty-one counties in the state of Mississippi in 1964.

In this day of instant information, there are written accounts from the students who journeyed from Antioch College, Syracuse, Oberlin, University of Michigan, and dozens of educational institutions across the United States, telling their experiences in my hometown, in my state. Their stories are shocking and don't seem at all to be true, yet they are. How could the good people of the Delta be so hate-filled and selfish to deny 65+ percent of the population, our neighbors and co-workers, the right to gather when and where they wished, to access the goods and services the government offered other citizens, and to participate in the greatest democracy the world had ever produced? I am still baffled and embarrassed that so few took a stand. If you don't know the particulars of Freedom Summer, it would be well worth looking up and studying. It is well documented. This story doesn't seem to be taught in schools. To me, it is a foundational story if one wants to understand the South during the Civil Rights struggle of the 1960s, and the dynamic between Black and white people. These days (2023) people on the other side of the issue have hung the term "Critical Race Theory" onto the truth, and have successfully vilified anyone who is in favor of teaching the true historical facts to our children. Teachers, professors, and other people of goodwill have lost jobs, been run out of public service positions, and off boards and commissions for daring to tell the unvarnished, unredacted truth.

The other thing that happened was that my grandmother's first cousin was Ross Barnett, the governor of Mississippi from 1960 to 1964. Although I'm never sure how these things work, I guess that made him my third cousin or second cousin once removed. At any rate, I shared DNA with the man. He is well known for blocking the door of Ole Miss when James Meredith tried to enroll as the first Black student in the school's history. Days of rioting ensued, and two people were killed. As an adult, I read the transcripts of the conversations between Cousin Ross and John F. Kennedy. I was so disappointed in both of them. I didn't feel that either one really cared about Meredith enrolling. They both were worried about how their supporters would react. Two consummate actors doing what they did best. It was a sorry time in America. But that's not the worst thing Ross Barnett did. During the first trial (there were ultimately three trials) of Medgar Evers' murderer, Byron de la Beckwith, Barnett walked into the courtroom, and as Mrs. Myrlie Evers testified about her husband's assassination before the all-white jury, Barnett stopped and shook Beckwith's hand for the world and the jury to see. That was in 1964. It would take a third trial in 1994 for a jury to convict Beckwith for the murder of the Civil Rights leader. He would spend the rest of his hate-filled life in prison. Barnett never apologized or atoned for that cruel and most unkind gesture. Mrs. Evers and her three young children left Mississippi.

Thomas Paine said, "Suspicion is the companion of mean souls and the bane of all good society." The government-funded Mississippi Sovereignty Commission and the White Citizens Council ruled Mississippi for decades, making laws, rigging elections, jailing protesters, and making what could be one of the finest places to live in this country into a joke, first in everything bad, last in everything good. Things have changed for the better in the past twenty years, but we've still got a long way to go.

The Book of Preston

David and me, 1984.

I had this friend, an opera singer I met in college and roomed with for a while, who later played in one of the bands I was in, and though he was a really talented musician, he never really grooved. He had that thing classical musicians possess, the fundamental belief that pop music was somehow less than and inferior to opera and classical music. We had discussions about this over the years with my contention being that classically trained musicians were all striving to sound alike, while most pop musicians were trying to be unique. I always felt that the emotion I heard and saw in opera singers was painstakingly choreographed and elaborately staged, and therefore false and empty as a distinctive, genuine human emotion. He tried to explain that pop music was simple, and therefore unimportant, the practitioners prancing and preening onstage to salve some missing thing in their being. That belief showed through his playing with the band. He was a talented harmonica player and a good percussionist, but his singing, while right on pitch and in meter, was either very stilted and uncool, or over-the-top dramatic. I could never believe in his performances. He and I talked about this a lot. His belief was that everything was a performance, and deserved the proper emotion. He would tell me that my performance was too off-hand and casual.

He moved to New York in the late 70s and tried to make it in the opera and on Broadway, but just didn't have the look. It seems he held every shitty job in NYC and lived usually for no more than a couple of months at a time with people he met through the theater or his busboy job. For a time he worked at a bill collection company who let him sleep in the breakroom. Just bizarre and sad things, and nothing ever seemed to work out. He gave it his all in New York but finally decided to try California. Another college friend made some vague offer of a place in the San Francisco Opera Company chorus. He was convinced that if he got in he could impress with his talent and finally make it to the big time. That job fizzled before it got off the ground, so he wandered the west coast for a while, living in rooming houses and basements, and more than once, the backstage of a theater, all the while trying to make it in the opera. Later, he got out of the music business all together, moved back to the South and began working a regular job, and for the first time in his life he had a little money and security. We talked on the phone often, and I saw him several times when he was traveling back and forth from California to Mississippi. Even though I knew he had lived a very tough life, a life of disappointment and desperation, I was proud of him for sticking to it. I loved his stories of sleeping in dressing rooms and cooking on a hot plate, picking up odd jobs as a short-order cook or a security guard, all the while going to auditions and helping to stage plays in community theaters. He is the kind of guy who should have written a book, but I don't think he had the awareness or insight to look at himself from without, and make an objective assessment of his life and his ramblings. He held the belief that art would take care of him.

When he went back to Mississippi in the early nineties, he worked for his brother installing satellite dishes. They were the new technology back then, and every shotgun shack and rundown mobile home in poor-ass Mississippi had one. He and his brother made pretty good money and he built a little house on his family land and did alright for himself. He had a big garden and some chickens running in the yard. I always assumed he had made a pact with himself to never be hungry again.

His dream was to start an opera company. In Como, Mississippi. As ridiculous as that might sound, he did it. But just as he was getting it started he was diagnosed with bone cancer. The cancer couldn't stop him. He was like a man possessed. He told me that after years of trying to make it happen somewhere else, he found that he had been meant to make it happen in a small town in Mississippi. He worked through the chemo treatments, writing letters, applying for grants, making phone calls. He did it all and inspired a group of local women to help. They made pimento cheese sandwiches and punch and cookies, and held fundraisers till they got where they wanted to be. He founded a company, mostly filled with singers from Memphis and Ole Miss, and performed operas in schools and in churches all over North Mississippi. Each year he had an Opera Under the Stars event in Como, which raised money for the coming season. Newspapers and television stations interviewed him, and things went well for three years till he got sick again and the doctors told him he couldn't take anymore chemo or radiation. Even after that death sentence, he never gave up. He worked that phone and computer up to the day he fell in his bathroom and had to be taken to the hospital.

I went to a museum the afternoon Preston died. I stayed all afternoon looking at the collection of old masters and second tier impressionist paintings, thinking that if I stayed maybe he wouldn't die. But I knew better, and when I walked out into the park after dawdling the afternoon away I knew he was gone. His sister had told me when I called earlier that day that he was barely conscious, but restless and wasn't expected to make it through the day. She had put Cat Stevens' "Tea for the Tillerman" CD in the player and placed his headphones on his chemo bald head. She said he calmed right down. That made me so sad. I knew how much he used to listen to that record when we were at Ole Miss and later when we lived together in Memphis, that it just about killed me to know that this was the last thing he'd ever listen to. It should have made me happy, but it didn't. I kept thinking that I could have helped him more, could have given him more money during those times when he was struggling. It's funny how when someone is in the middle of something, no matter how tough or bleak it seems, they land in one of two ways and rarely in the middle. If they are a person grounded in optimism, they will say things like, "Oh, it's okay, things are bound to get better. I'm alright." If they're a pessimist, it's more like, "Damn, I can't do anything right. Everything I do blows up in my face. I'm just going to quit trying." Preston was an optimist up to the end. I think about him often, and I've increasingly come to appreciate the honesty he and I shared about our understanding of art and music. In another life he is on the Broadway stage six days a week and twice on Sundays.

My Father's Voice

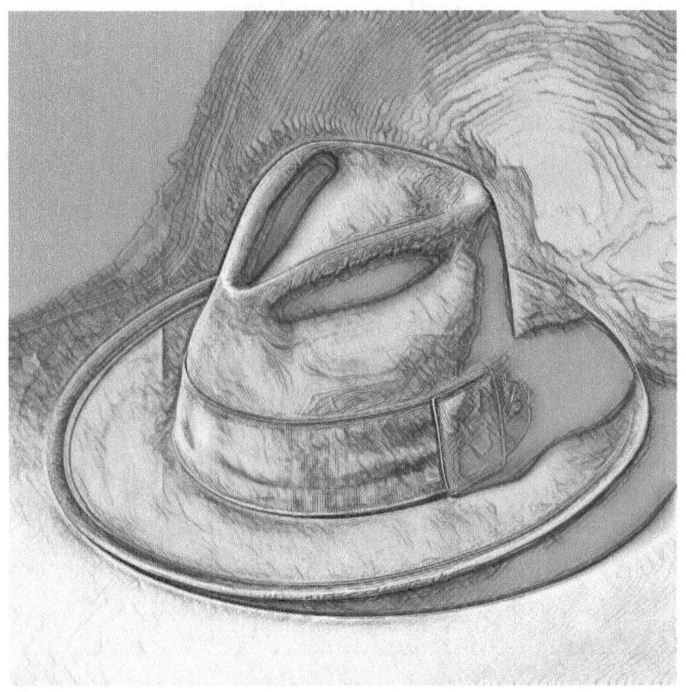

Sometimes for a moment, a split second, I can no longer hear my father's voice. Neither the timbre nor the rhythm or any specific thing he said. I can see him perfectly, in a rush of frames my mind has organized into a slide-show or a movie flashback. Always the sunglasses, the fedora in the 40s and 50s, the cap in the 70s and 80s, but always some kind of covering. I can smell the Vitalis hair oil, the Aqua Velva or Old Spice,

Chesterfields and Double Mint chewing gum, a hint of Early Times or Yellowstone bourbon underlining the whole thing. His boots were always Wellingtons, straight out of the Sears Roebuck catalog, black, unadorned, and polished to a shiny black brilliance. Later, when Sears stopped carrying the boots, he moved to regular cowboy boots but they never looked quite right. He was a khakis man, starched, creased and stiff, and he hitched his pants a little before sitting down. He also cussed a good bit, but within reason and often with a caveat. If women were around he would say something like, "Now, that sumbitch, 'scuse me ladies, that sumbitch doesn't know what he's talking about," getting to say it twice while maintaining some imagined level of decorum.

As I wander this path of memory thinking I've lost his voice forever, it somehow jumpstarts my brain and I can hear him again in a flash. His cadence and resonance are planted firmly in my ear, and I remember how he said certain words, things I never hear anymore except for a few really old ladies I know from the Delta. That accent is nearly gone. Shelby Foote had it, and my father had hints of it.

He was a driver of backroads, mainly because he was always at some level or another of inebriation, but he also liked to ride and look, comment on crops, stop at country stores for a beer, salted peanuts, or a pack of nabs, which I still call them today. You know those little crackers with peanut butter? Nabs, I guess, because they were made by the Nabisco company. The National Biscuit Company.

He was a little self-conscious, while at the same time being a little haughty. His somewhat patrician upbringing wouldn't let him get right down with the rednecks, but he laughed at their antics and played along with their foolishness. He liked stories of the worst of them, retelling how so-and-so had gotten thrown out of the house for coming in drunk too many nights in a row, or how the fellow who owned the Monkey Store in Greenville had been cast out of the house and went to sleep in the monkey cage outside the store, where on this particular night the temperature got down below freezing, and the man stole all the covers, and the monkeys froze. He also liked the mynah bird at the Percy Store on highway 61 who would wait till you were in the store for a minute, then say something like "well, sonuvabitch" or "hey baldy," or "well kiss my ass." He thought that was the funniest thing. I think he also liked these stories because they normalized his behavior and made him feel that this was how everyone acted.

When we would go to Port Gibson to see his brother, he loved telling the story of the time he and his best friend, Al Jay, got a ride to Jackson with a route salesman, whose daddy was a judge and old family friend. They went to buy a bicycle. It was 1933, and he had saved his money for a year to get the new 'wheel,' as Al called it. The route salesman picked Daddy and Al up at Bearden's Store in Pattison, which was owned by Daddy's brother, John. It's important to mention here that Al was three months older than my father, which carried more weight between the two of them than the fact that Al was Black. Not to say that my father didn't take advantage of his position as resident White guy. It seems that he and Al had been virtually inseparable their whole lives, thirteen years. Al saddled the horses every morning and they rode the short distance to the school where he waited patiently all day for his friend/employer to be free in the afternoon. What a bizarre arrangement this was. Daddy always said that Al was the smarter of the two of them, and was more physically gifted and agile. I'm sure they had spent days and weeks planning this adventure to get the bicycle.

They rode to Jackson and spent the night at the old judge's house. I cannot imagine what the meal or sleeping arrangements would have been in 1933. I'm sure Al ate in the kitchen and probably slept on a pallet on the floor of the bedroom where my father slept. The story went that early the next morning they were driven to a business that sold bicycles. Probably a Western Auto or maybe a Sears Roebuck store, where my father parted with his hard-earned money and purchased the ride of his dreams.

As he related the story, they rode the bicycle out of Jackson, on the paved streets and what he called hard roads, Daddy pedaling and Al on the back, till they got to the edge of town and Highway 18 turned to gravel. They quickly saw that riding double was not going to be easy on the gravel. It was decided that one would ride the bike and the other would run alongside, then they would switch places for the next mile or so. It seems that this plan worked okay for a while, but the times began to get longer and longer for the lucky pedaler, and the runner was getting increasingly frustrated, and lagged far behind. At this point my father decided that since it was his bicycle, he would be the only one riding and that Al could run alongside or walk, his choice, till they got back to Pattison, which was some forty five miles ahead. This plan worked nicely for the first few miles, but by the time Al walked up to my father sitting under a tree, grinning, and saying something like, "Where the hell you been? I ain't waiting for you like this all day. It'll take us till midnight to get back to the house," he had had enough. My father said Al got a crazy look in his eye and jumped on him and they wrestled like bear cubs till they were both sweaty and spent.

This fight sequence apparently went on another couple of times through the morning and early afternoon till they reached a paved road. They were back in business. They decided that whoever was riding in front would put his feet on top of the backseat rider's feet and they could both pedal and really make some time. On through the afternoon and into the evening they fairly flew through crossroads and hamlets till they saw the lights of Pattison. My father's brother, John, was just closing the store when they rode up. "Well, I was wondering if we would see you two before sunup tomorrow. How'd you do?" The boys looked at each other, and just as my father was about to tell him about the long day and the fights, Al said, "We did just fine, Mr. John, just fine."

I don't know how many times my father recounted this story, but he always had a tear in his eye when he remembered what Al said. And as I think of it these many years later, I don't think I ever saw him be emotional or cry about anything else.

The Fluid Nature of the Truth

(A time capsule from 2004)

Last week I had the good fortune of being a presenter at the second annual Delta Symposium at the University of Memphis. Roughly two hundred people of all stripes, interests, political persuasions, ages, and body types attended this daylong event. The common thread that ran through the crowd was that each person had a keen interest in the history and development of the Mississippi Delta. More accurately, a keen enough interest to part with the fifty-dollar enrollment fee.

Our social and economic heritage in Memphis and Shelby County is inexorably linked to the Delta, to the point that many of us feel no more than a slight allegiance to the state of Tennessee, but rather feel that we are simply living in the capital of the Delta. Greenville, Mississippi writer David Cohn probably had no idea that his words would ring nostalgically true some seventy years after he wrote them: "The Delta begins in the lobby of the Peabody Hotel in Memphis and ends on Catfish Row in Vicksburg." The reality of this statement, along with the fact of Blues and rock 'n roll, is the cornerstone of who we are, what we market, and why people continue to visit our part of the world in ever-increasing numbers. People around the world are fascinated with the South in general and the Delta specifically. Walk around downtown Memphis at any time day or night and you're likely to see dozens of people who "aren't from around here" checking us out.

Fifty years ago, there were very few situations or places where Black and white people could congregate without the risk of being jailed, beaten, or worse. A free exchange of ideas and opinions between the races was unheard of, and certainly the idea of a public event touting that would have been insane, and that's the truth. But our truth changed. Just as the idea of allowing a woman to vote changed in the 1920s, just as the idea of banning 5- and 6-year-old children from working in the cotton mills changed in the early 20th century, and any number of other scenarios that seem perfectly ridiculous to us in our current enlightened state. Which issues will our grandchildren and great-grandchildren look back on, shake their heads and wonder what we were thinking here in the early days of the 21st century?

My two youngest children graduated from high school last year, and the only bit of advice I felt compelled to offer was this: "I give you permission to change your mind. Whatever political, social, occupational, or religious idea you are clinging to with such fervor today, you can change without so much as a raised eyebrow from your old man." Too many times we paint ourselves into a philosophical corner and feel compelled to defend a position that is either ill-conceived or developed through some faulty, vague, or downright mean logic. (Can you say talk radio?) While this is most commonly associated with young people who are just testing their ideological wings, we adults are not immune. Therefore, I propose a day of your choosing each year to challenge your list of opinions, prejudices, and beliefs. The good news is that most of them will prove to be sound, but for those of us who need to tweak our list, the payoff is enormous. We become better parents, neighbors, and citizens. A wise man once said that we can deny everything, except that we have the possibility of being better. This could be a start.

Willie the Red

It's odd how some memories grow with time to encompass bigger themes and deeper patterns while others slip into the narcosis of nostalgia. Time has a way of changing everything, and who knows where we would wind up in our thinking if the average lifespan were 200 years instead of a mere 70y-something. It is in looking back that we see how far we have come. This journey in memory has caused me to wince at some of the notions and assumptions I walked around with.

I am blessed with a memory mostly devoid of nostalgia, and scenes play out exactly as they did many years ago when they happened for the first time. The difference is in my understanding. I am constantly embarrassed and sometimes shocked by my naivete and willingness to talk myself into enterprises that are foolhardy at best and verging on criminal, or certainly dangerous, at worst. In setting down these stories I have chosen to tell the truth about a time in my life when I was armed with only faint notions about how the world worked and how little control I wielded over my existence.

I see now that I gravitated to outsiders and marginalized groups of people. There was some strange comfort in not fitting in with the mainstream of American life. These beliefs made for odd friendships and shaky alliances as I moved through the world. And with those caveats, I offer you the story of Willie the Red.

"Hey man, you ready? Let's go. You wanna smoke a J before we go?"

I didn't mind if I did, and ten minutes later we were tooling down Alcy Road in the yellow Ranchero, 8 track blaring, windows down, headed for Whitehaven to pick up a load of gently used dump truck tires. We were poised for greatness, emboldened by marijuana seeds and stems and Bob Seger, perfectly ready to talk business to the many people who surely were looking for tires for recapping. It was a good day.

I heard the Ford Ranchero pull into the cove before I saw it. I had been waiting there by myself for an hour, and I was a little pissed because this whole episode had begun the day before with him talking to me about getting serious about life, and getting a job, or at least making some money. He made me swear that I would be ready bright and early the next day. He had a plan, and it was going to take some running around to get everything together to make it work. It seemed that his uncle had some dump truck tires in his backyard, and they were prime for being recapped. That is, they were completely worn out from hauling asphalt around the South, "paving" driveways, or bouncing along farm roads looking for barns that needed "one more" lightning rod to protect the farm from the coming onslaughts of killer lightning bolts. My guess is that the uncle made the offer of the tires just to give Willie something to keep him busy and off his payroll. Most truck tires were "recycled" that way. Still are. They would grind off the old tread and vulcanize a fresh tread, and hope it wouldn't fly off within the first week or so.

Willie was one of those guys who would look at you through the ever-present cloud of marijuana smoke and say something like, "You know man, I'm gonna get into reading." Or "I'm gonna get me a 'partment." I never knew quite how to respond. He was a Gypsy, (nowadays they're known as "Roma") and everybody knew that Gypsies were a breed apart. They rarely went to school beyond the seventh grade, and they thought that we "gorgers" were simple beings, unschooled in the art of commerce. They thought us persuadable, inexperienced, and easily exploitable. All of this was certainly true when it came to the other gypsies we knew: Little Richard, Monk, Brother Budgie, Billie-bake-the-cake, Ace. Willie was different. Even the source of his name set him apart from his cousins, who were typical Romani, dark-skinned with dark hair. Willie had hair the color of a new penny, freckles, and a simple, bemused countenance that distinguished him from his kinsmen. I thought of Willie as the simple Gypsy, the dimmest of bulbs in the gypsy firmament, and an unspoken but bitter disappointment to his large family, principally an elderly mother who lived in a crowded trailer park on Bellevue Blvd., a couple of miles north of Graceland. Willie was Gomer, or maybe Goober of the Gypsies.

The Gypsies had a well-earned reputation for scams and intricate plots to separate an otherwise intelligent person from their money. Paving driveways (with no more than ⅛" inch of asphalt) was the easiest and most lucrative of the ploys, followed by barn painting (who knew a huge barn could be painted with one gallon of paint?), and lightning rod installation (one rod every six feet is the government recommendation.) They were also great practitioners of cock fighting; many of them widely known for their rigorous training of the fowls for Saturday night contests that would generate thousands of dollars in bets and side bets.

But Willie was cool. He always had a goofy smile on his face, he dressed in the latest "hippie" fashions, ran around with a bunch of stunningly beautiful Roma girls who wouldn't give me the time of day, even though I tried my hardest to impress or get their attention in some way. They weren't having any of it. Willie, using his ever-present line, burst in the door that morning, popped an Elvis karate move and said, "On the scene, boys!" even though I was the only person at the house.

The House 1972

Our family road trip to Mountain View, Arkansas, 1972.
Front, l to r, Mary Alice, Debby, Kim, Carl, Robert. Back, Charlie, Marsha,
Robby, Willy, George, David.

The Dawnwood Cove house was a two bedroom duplex in a transitional neighborhood. We sweet-talked the lady into renting it to us. We were a ragged band of hippies, nine of us, scratching a living together with menial jobs and day labor at Manpower. I was currently unemployed and the rent was due. My part was $22 a month, a deal that I struck with the other residents. My bedroom was the living room floor. I won't go into our daily routines, but, as my uncle would say, there were multiple lines of monkey business going on in and around that duplex.

Willie and I cruised our way down Elvis Presley Boulevard. Willie's uncle, as it turned out, indeed had a bunch of tires in his backyard. We loaded as many as the small bed on the Ranchero could hold, and headed out for Third Street, where there were tire stores galore. The first place we stopped was a big place at Brooks Road and Third Street, 61 Tire Company. We walked into the office and I, with my best businessman impression, walked to the counter and said something like, "I know there's a shortage of tires for recapping, and we happen to have some of the best you've ever seen, right out here in the truck. How much are you fellas paying?" I was cousin-talking him to the best of my ability.

The guy didn't even look up, and said, "Not buying any tires today."

I jumped right back in, "What day do you buy tires, sir?"

"Ain't looking for any tires," without ever looking up. Had he looked up he would have seen a 21-year-old businessman with hair down to his shoulders, and bell-bottomed Levis. Not exactly a young executive on the move. Willie looked crestfallen. We walked back out to the truck and by the time he cranked it up he was back to his old positive self.

"I knew those fuckin' guys weren't gonna buy any tires. I could tell when we walked in that joint. Let's go down to this place where I know they buy tires. Them sonofabitches didn't know their ass from a hole in the ground." Willie gunned the Ranchero and laid a little rubber getting out of the parking lot.

He grinned at his rebellious act.

"Hey, let's stop and get some donuts." He giggled that familiar laugh, his eyes bloodshot, and his mind now on a donut or three. "I don't have but a dollar."

"That'll get us 5. We'll cut one in half."

"Yeah, I've got the munchies. That is some good weed. Where'd you get it?"

Willie got serious. "I can't tell you man. My cousin got it from his cousin in Mayfield. It's Mexican."

"So you just told me."

"No I didn't. I didn't say his name." Willie looked at me suspiciously.

"Which cousin?" I was fucking with him.

"Shorty," he said before he could stop himself. I laughed out loud. He gunned it down Third Street.

"Oh, man, that's a cool shirt. Wanna sell it?" I asked.

"No man, I bought it at U.S. Male. I bought it on time, brother." Clearly proud of himself. "It was seven dollars. I got some elephant bells, too."

"You gonna pay 'em?"

"Yeah, just as soon as we get these tires sold."

And on it went through the morning. At our next stop, the guy actually came out and looked at the tires before he told us he wasn't interested. I thought I was getting better at my sales pitch, and Willie agreed, but at the third place the man shook his head and said, "Don't need 'em, don't want 'em." We pressed on. On Bellevue, I chatted up the man behind the counter and coaxed him out to look at the tires. "Sorry fellas, we don't do much recappin' these days." Lamar and Airways was a bust, even after offering the manager a great deal on the tires. Just as we got back on the street Willie pulled over in the Loeb's BBQ parking lot. He put the truck in park and looked out the side window for a few seconds.

He sighed and turned to me. He had a funny look on his face, almost like he was about to cry. "Hey, man, I don't want to piss you off or anything, but I need to say something."

"Okay, what?" I had no idea what was coming.

"Man, the deal is, well, it's not like you did anything wrong or anything, but you don't know how to talk to people. You ain't a Gypsy, and that ain't your fault, but we know how to sell people stuff. We know how to talk people into buying stuff from us. I hope you don't get mad, man, but you're kinda fucking me up."

"Hey, man, that's the last thing I wanna do. I need to make some money. That's all I've been trying to do, man, talk to these guys 'cause they're all gorgers, too, right?"

"Man, yeah man, it's just not the same thing. Let me go in the next place and you stay in the truck, okay? You're not a Gypsy, there ain't nothing wrong with that. You just don't know." "Sure, I'm just looking to make some money. My rent's due." But it did hurt my feelings.

We drove in silence and pulled into 61 Tires. Before Willie got out of the truck he apologized again, and said this was going to be alright when we got our money. I nodded, and he walked in. I was expecting him to walk back out in ten seconds, redeeming my gorger self-respect, but he didn't. A minute turned to three, and three turned to ten, and I'm steadily trying to rationalize why that dumbass was having success when I had failed miserably. Finally, Willie walked out and got in the truck.

"Well, did you sell 'em?" I asked, trying not to sound giddy in the least, though I was somewhere between butt-hurtedness and relief.

Willie cranked the car and pulled slowly forward toward the grease rack inside the garage. There was a guy guiding us onto the rack, and Willie was looking at him intently. He still hadn't said a word.

"Hey man, did you sell the tires? What did he say?"

Willie stared straight ahead, stopped the truck and put it in park. He still wouldn't look at me. He said, "He sold me a set of tires."

"He what?"

"He sold me a set of tires," he said shamelessly.

"He sold YOU a set of tires? How the fuck did that happen?"

"They have this new deal where you don't have to put any money down, and you can pay ten payments and have 'em paid off in less than a year. It's a pretty good deal."

"Wait a minute, you signed something saying you were gonna pay them ten payments? You don't have any money!"

"I know, man, I'm not gonna really pay for 'em." I was so pissed at him I could've gotten out of the car and walked home.

We drove in relative silence down to Whitehaven to Willie's uncle's house. We were unloading the tires behind a backyard shed when his uncle rounded the corner and said, "Hey, boys, how'd you do?"

Willie said, "Pretty good. We got some good leads. A bunch of people liked the tires, they just don't need them right this second. They said come back next week."

The uncle looked at me, "Hey, why don't y'all just go ahead and buy the tires from me and you won't have to come all the way down here every time you want to sell some? I'll make you a good deal. Those are some good tires. Good for recapping, you know."

Willy Bearden

The Nickel Thief

Daddy and his girlfriend, Ruby

The past is always bubbling just below the surface of the present, ready to boil over, or to ooze out of the cracks and crevices to remind us it's still here. What did Mr. Faulkner say? "The past is never dead. It's not even past."

What of my father? Dead now for thirty five years, the faintest of memory to but a few. Even when he was alive, he was an old man living in a mobile home on the roadside, deep in the country, still haunted by his own past, his own failings, regrets and delusions. Do I owe him some apology? Do I owe him anything? He, who never wanted me; do I owe him some unspoken tribute, some acknowledgment? DNA is a strong determinant of what will be, but does it demand respect? Does it possess a pull like gravity? The story I wrote was like the many things I've written that have yet to see the light of day. What of the truth there, locked away for years in a tomb of paper, a vault of words? What of the grievances and resentments that have powered my own life, locked beneath so much hostility and hurt that it is near impossible to sort out? The truth itself, it just floats on in memory, defined and redefined by each of us until it either makes us feel good, vindicated, and whole, or remains a waking nightmare, a wound that will never fully heal, the thing your mind knows not to go towards because nothing but trouble hides there.

I've wanted and ached to go back and apologize to him. There was a moment he gave up, at least on us: a moment sitting at the ridiculous stately round oak dining table that had been his parents and grandparents, so out of place in our little house; a moment I turned my nose up at what he had spent the afternoon cooking. So unlike him to ever cook or think in those nurturing ways about us, but I was only eleven, and I was sick with the flu. Everything smelled funny to me that day, and I said it to him, "This smells bad." The hurt showed on his face. The next night when old man Harms burst in the door and stormed back to his bedroom and fired him was the other moment when he quit, gave up, surrendered. How could I expect him to be anything other than what he was? How can we expect anything from another person? Someone told me once that hurt people hurt people, but we expect our parents to be something more, something better. The trauma reverberates down through the generations, manifesting itself in the most common of the maladies: selfishness, alcoholism, addiction. Where does it end? I wanted it to end with me.

The other thing was that I felt a deep sense of shame for something I had done to him when I was a kid. It had played in the back of my mind for years, usually at times when I should have been experiencing joy for an accomplishment or pride for something well done, it was lurking there to stop me in my tracks. To remind me that even with all the good and the success, I was still that little thief. You see, I used to look at his collection of Indian head nickels. They were in the box that his .22 caliber pistol had come in, a nice, faux leather box lined with green felt. The box was heavy with the nickels, and smelled musty and old. I'd sit there on their bed, alone in the house, looking for the oldest one, finding lots from the thirties and forties, a few from the twenties and even fewer still from the teens. I was fascinated by the coins, and somehow proud that he had a collection. Then one day I took one. It was a late thirties one that was in pretty bad shape so I knew it wasn't worth much, but I felt the sting of shame when I paid for the 10 cookies I got at Mr. Brown's store. The next day I took another nickel, and the day after that, another.

There were only a few times I remember actually having a conversation with him. That day he drove up late in the afternoon when I was burning the trash in the barrel beside our house, and walked over to me, cigarette hanging out of his mouth, "You been stealing my nickels?"
"No, Daddy." I lied.
"Where did you spend them?"
"I didn't take them. I swear."
"Yes you did. They were in my pistol box."
"I'm sorry. I'll pay you back." Tears were beginning to stream down my face.

"You're a thief." He began walking toward the house. "I never thought I'd raise a goddam thief," he muttered. He didn't say a word to me for a long time after that.

Preacher

When the party ends.

I became an ordained minister, a monk in the Universal Life Monastery, about eight years ago when it was decided that my girlfriend's sister and her boyfriend should get married at their engagement party. Take a second if you need to let that sink in. I think it was a brilliant ploy for people who didn't want to get pulled back and forth about where to get married, how much to spend, who to invite. Just do it at the engagement party and call it done. My investiture was one of those internet things where you pay fifty bucks and they send you a laminated card with Clergy written on it, an official looking certificate stating that you're ordained by the Universal Life Church, and a little dashboard sign if you might have the need to park at a hospital or some other official place. I may or may not have used that privilege since becoming ordained.

So far, I've married five couples, all related in some odd way to my now brother-in-law, Marlin. His Mom and stepfather (Linda and Jerry) were my second couple, then a couple (Kay and Ellis) his mom met in a doctor's office, who knew me from Rolling Fork; next was Marlin's niece, Lauren and her husband Pat, then the out-of-the-blue couple I married with only their dogs in attendance, and finally Ryan and Kayla, who are Marlin's friends. The ceremonies have been very touching, and have made me feel like I was doing exactly the right thing. At this writing, all are still together and thriving.

My favorite occurrence has to be when I married Ellis and Kay, the woman from Rolling Fork, I was asked to stay for cake and refreshments. I was happy to oblige, and while the festivities were taking place, I was referred to as "the Preacher" several times by her friends and neighbors who were in attendance. I politely told the first lady who had said something like, "Y'all let the preacher get some cake and punch," that I was not a preacher, but she just looked at me funny and kept serving cake. So, after that, I let it go, and kind of basked in being called the preacher. I fancy myself a good monk, spreading marital bliss far and wide. I hope to do more of this kind of work in the future. It is heartening, and a bit ironic that I'm batting .1000 in the marriage game. All of my people are still married. Looks like I tie a pretty tight knot. I love it when people are full to the brim with hope and happiness and cake.

Memorial Day

My mother, Virginia Bernice Wright, her brother, M.O. Wright, Jr., and their sister, Maudelle Wright, c.1925. Photo by Claudine Nester

This is my Memorial Day. They say a person dies twice. The first time is when they cease to breathe and are no longer among us in the physical world. The second and final time a person dies is when the last person who knew their story says their name for the final time. When I wrote the foreword to this book many years ago, I said that if I thought a little I could probably recreate the list of people I've known who are no longer here. After everything else was done, I allowed myself a couple of days to think down the corridors of my memory to the people I knew, had interaction with, looked into their eyes, and could tell a story about.

Some, maybe many, names will be misspelled. That doesn't bother me. What gives me solace is the fact that I can tell you a story about any person on this list. In some way, great or small, they had an impact on my life and I'm glad to have known them, known their stories. In the end, I say their names out loud.

Virginia Trigleth
Joe Trigleth
Eugene Trigleth
Gaines Bearden
Maudell Wright Fox
Anne Sevier-Hartline
Dot Helton
Andy Helton
Hattie Lee Trigleth
Maude Barnett Wright
Murphy Odus Wright
Robert Wright
Homer Wright
Alice Barnett
Roberta Wright Wilson
Dr. Bryant R. Wilson
Mathew G. Bearden
Ruby Thompson
Walter Williams
Cheryl J. Bearden
Stanley Johnson
Bill Johnson
Frances Johnson
Andy Branham
Paul Averwater
Robert Waldon
Ron Watkins
Rodney Heigle
Larry Brent Wilson
Shirley Stewart
Frank Swords
David Cousar
Ruby Walker
Mae Henry Wright
Peggy Wilson

Gus Wilson
Leila S. Perkins
Bernice Phillips
J.B. Phillips
David Phillips
Lavelle Trigleth
Derwin Trigleth
Joseph Allen Trigleth
Ham Smythe
Marvell Thomas
William Lee Dees
George Cates
Sue Reid Williams
Fred Blake
Betty Blake
Marjorie Larrimore
Maurice Larrimore
Eldridge Wright
Evelyn Bernard
Bob Acree
Terry Wayne Mayo
Tracey Prigmore
Samantha Prigmore
Dudley Davis
Ron Michael Hughes
Knox Phillips
David Durrett
Lance Young
George Vergos
Adam Pongetti
Fred Armistead
Daryl Clark
Robbie Carr
Eula B. Cummings
Faron Cummings

Alice Brantley
Shelby Foote
Leola Lawrence
Russell George
Miriam DeCosta Willis
John Harkins
Hite McLean
Sid Selvidge
Ernest Withers
Jack Moore
Butch Laurie
Jon Poulin
Irvin Salky
Nannie Rives Trusty
Mary Rives Forgey
Florence Leffler
Carsie Bozeman
Bobby Rutherford
Bennett Wood
Cecil Vick
Mike Vick
Jackie Ware
Nick Giardino
Helen Giardino
Earnest Withers
Samantha Barns
Charlie Harmon
Jerry Hayes
Pierre Kimsey
Russ Abernathy
Frank Robison
Elizabeth Robison
Doug Barlow
Rev. H.D. Dennis
Margaret Dennis

Jeff Hays
Columbus Flood
Jimmy Harrison
B.B. Cunningham
Terry Cox
Melvin Jones
Rufus Thomas
Gladys Miller
Willie Hammond
Polly Hammond
Huey Thornhill
Jack Grundfest
Cecil Blakeney
Louise Bishop
Jimmy Thornhill
Carolyn Thornhill
Cindy Thornhill
Robert White
Fred Jabbour
Sarah Jabbour
Joe Burney
Naomi Burney
Georgia Gray
Bo Hinton
Carolyn Truesdale
Burt Truesdale
Rae Nell Hunter
Marshall Jones
Miriam Perry
Little Larry
Buck Roebuck
Bubba Parker
Carson Holloman
Johnny Dungan
Kevin Scott

Janella Jones	Johnny Dribben
Terry Joe Jones	Buddy Thornhill
Angeline Jones	Kitty Chambliss
Buck Jones	Bobbi Clark
Carl Thornhill	Evelyn Freeny
Jimmy Helms	Leroy Dunaway
Sydney Smith	Robert A. Rochelle
David Tully Johnson	Ronie Hurst
Darby Johnson	Ethel Hurst
Mike Abel	James Hand, Jr.
Debbie Red	Charles Hand
Steve McClain	Fred Hinton
Miss Petty Meek Kelly	Lawrence Carter
Herman Glazer	H.G. Fenton
Leon Waldon	C.D. Crawford
Fay Brown Waldon	Bebe Rodgers
H.A. Cain	Grace Young
Sophie Cain	Lawrence Mullins
Ruth Baggett	C.T. Seale
Hal DeCell	Imogene Carter
Carolyn DeCell	Dooley Lee
Coleman Clements	Ollie Kyzar
B.B. King	V.A. Snuggs
Terry Tharp	Eula Lee Snuggs
James Hoffman	Imojean Majure
C. J. Perkins	Clayton Wright
Spencer Powers	Murphy O. Wright, Jr.
George Wallace	Gordon Hoxie
Johnny Boston	Ray Mosby
Inman Denton	Happy Blair
Mary Denton	Eudora Welty
Georgia F. Sharbrough	Mike Parker
James Hand Carter	Don Miller
Don Norris	Ann Miller
Glenn Griffin	Janie Moore

Dr. Maghee Moore
Robert Morganfield
Alice Bailey
Ronnie Bearman
Roosevelt Bailey
Ora Lee Stewart
Jack Shults
Louie Prestiani
Howard Stevens
Sally Stevens
John Pippin
Mary Lynn Pippin
Wayne Cole
Henry Phelps
Pat Walker
Ed Shropshire
Emily Shropshire
Ryland Shropshire
David Ewing
Sam Hobbs
Orla Brown
Mary Brown
Pat Brown Hoffman
Ryan Grayson
Buster Herman
Frances Moore
Johnny French
Billy Freeny
Leland Weissinger
Bubba Lawler
Harris Terry
D.K. Stevens
H.J. Winslow
Mildred Jones
David 'HotShot' Jones

Bobby Blackley
Sally Hunter Blackley
Allen Chase
Cauley Chase
Marion Chase
Harry Rivers
Shirley McCoy
B.B. Scott
Howard Lang
Rush Clements
Dot Graft Pitts
Jack Pitts
Billy Touchberry
Sandra Caselli
Tommy Courtney
Joe Bob Barnhill
Juanita Tullos
Blaine Baker
Buddy Morgan
Willie Brassell
Jack Vaughn
Nat Berkley
Harry Estes
Lemmie Isbell
John Kilzer
Don Windham
Glen Windham
Owen Hoffman
Eddie Strickland
Lloyd Brizendine
George Brooks
Marybelle Ferrell
Sammy Smithart
Bennie Lee Clark
Darna Mae Clark

Kenneth Burns
Bobby Burns
Bobbi Chambliss
Eleanor Hardin
Mrs. Cobb
Pop Cobb
Sam Jue
Tommy Percival
Danny Martin
Sam Rosenthal
Bessie Rosenthal
Glen Baker
Alice Baker
Hubert Tucker
Lorraine Beaver
Leroy Miller
Harry Simmons
Sue Quarm
Gordon Quarm
Thad Jordan
Mickie Jordan
Betty Montgomery
Monty Montgomery
Ben Lamensdorf
Betty Lee Lamensdorf
Sam Lamensdorf
SusieBelleLamensdorf
Bloom Carroll
Charlie Clark
Joe Hicks
Dot Fleeman
Ed Danzig
Louie Danzig
Lynn Phillips
Maurice Phillips

Curtis Tircuit
Ella Jo Tircuit
Jimmy McCaa
Boob McCaa
Bertha McCaa
Mimi Ariago
Betty Ann Clark
Onnie Latham
Hoggie Latham
Hayward Lovorn
Mac Aden
Buddy Burrus
Marvin Burrus
Jimmy Burrus
Billy Burrus
Lewis Vandevender
Otha Renfro
Terrell Reese
Ann Stephens
Jim Turner
Carl Cauthen
Sherry Cauthen
Mac Sorrells
Edna Sorrells
Ann Culpepper
Dorothy Cortright
Geraldine Atchley
Diana Davis
Leon Davis
Janet Brizendine
John Bearden
Laura Ellen Bearden
Elizabeth B. Gates
Jeanne Bearden
Robert Bearden

Norman Bearden
Florence Trevilion
Thomas Trevilion
John Trevilion
James Floyd Wright
Harold Wright
M.O. Wright
Mary Julia Wright
Ray Arrington
Ruby Arrington
Pervie Arrington
Loren Larrimore
Zane Melmed
Bill Murray
Adam Geary
Cato Walker
Duane Griffin
Jim "Stump" Elliott
Leo "Tater Red" Allred
Bob Durdin

*My uncle, Murphy O. Wright, Jr. was killed on March 24, 1945, as the Allies
crossed the Rhine River in Holland.
The war ended six weeks later.*

And what of stories left untold?
Doomed to molder in darkened closets
and forgotten backyards. Never tendered
the breath of life, the opportunity to shine,
the glory to grow old and be
passed among those who would never
know the first teller. Would we be
poorer still, or the not knowing
some comfort or mercy of omission? But perhaps
left to drift in flutterous commotion,
become the gift for one, the savior
of another, the inspiration of the waiting.

Willy Bearden

I sincerely hope this book spoke to you in some way. There is power, and maybe a bit of magic when people share their experiences with others. As human beings we are imbued with limitless possibilities, and the journey is made easier and more meaningful when we make it with people we love and respect. If you enjoyed this book, please consider writing a review with your honest impressions on Amazon, Goodreads, or the platform of your choosing. Your feedback is incredibly valuable for helping independent authors like us reach a wider audience.

Mississippi Hippie is available in hardback, soft cover, e-book, and audiobook at:
www.mississippihippiebook.com
Or where fine books are sold.
For more resources and events, please visit www.willybearden.com

If you'd like to contact me, I'm reachable at willyb@aol.com

©2024 William Bearden, all rights reserved.

About the Author

Willy Bearden is a Memphis filmmaker, author, photographer, and producer, whose passion for storytelling has propelled him throughout his long career. Born and raised in the heart of the Deep Delta, Rolling Fork, Mississippi, Bearden's upbringing instilled in him a profound appreciation for the rich, yet bizarre cultural tapestry of the American South.

A prolific filmmaker, Bearden has left a mark on the documentary landscape with his insightful and evocative films. From "Visualizing the Blues" to "Carroll Cloar: Life and Art" to "Elmwood Cemetery," his work delves deep into the essence of Southern culture, shedding light on the vibrant traditions and storied history of the region. His documentaries, including "A History of Memphis Garage Bands" and "The View from Adams Avenue," serve as poignant reminders of the diverse musical and cultural landscapes that define Memphis and the South.

Beyond the realm of filmmaking, Bearden's influence extends to museum projects that celebrate the soulful essence of the South. His dedication to preserving and showcasing the region's cultural heritage is evident in his contributions to institutions such as The Blues Hall of Fame, The Grammy Museum/Mississippi, and The Elvis Presley Birthplace Museum, among others.

As an author, Bearden's literary works offer compelling insights into Southern history and culture. His books, including "Elmwood Cemetery", "Cotton, From Southern Fields to the Memphis Market", "Memphis Blues, Birthplace of a Music Tradition," and "Overton Park", serve as essential chronicles of the region's past, present, and future. "Mississippi Hippie" is his long-awaited memoir, sharing the true stories of his upbringing and hitch-hiking wanderings as a young man in the late 1960s and early 70s.

With over three decades of experience in live event production, Bearden is a seasoned veteran in bringing stories to life on stage. From producing the Blues Music Awards to orchestrating the annual Blues Hall of Fame inductions, he continues to craft unforgettable experiences.

In addition to his creative endeavors, Bearden is a respected speaker, sharing his passion for Southern culture at dozens of public speaking engagements each year. His contributions to the arts have been recognized with numerous accolades, including the Blues Foundation's *Keeping the Blues Alive Award*, the *Paul Coppock Award for Outstanding Contributions to West Tennessee History*, and he is the recipient of the *2011 Distinguished Achievement Award in the Creative and Performing Arts* presented by the College of Communication and Fine Arts at the University of Memphis.

Willy Bearden's remarkable journey from the Deep Delta to the forefront of Southern storytelling is a testament to his unwavering dedication to preserving and honoring the authentic voice of the American South.

www.ingramcontent.com/pod-product-compliance
Lightning Source LLC
Chambersburg PA
CBHW051310130726
47987CB00004B/1736